NORTH WEST INSPIRATIONS 1999

Edited by

Steve Twelvetree

First published in Great Britain in 1999 by
ANCHOR BOOKS
Remus House,
Coltsfoot Drive,
Woodston,
Peterborough, PE2 9JX
Telephone (01733) 898101

All Rights Reserved

Copyright Contributors 1999

HB ISBN 1 85930 684 5
SB ISBN 1 85930 689 6

FOREWORD

Anchor Books is a small press, established in 1992, with the aim of promoting readable poetry to as wide an audience as possible.

We hope to establish an outlet for writers of poetry who may have struggled to see their work in print.

The poems presented here have been selected from many entries. Editing proved to be a difficult task and as the Editor, the final selection was mine.

Anchor books North-West Inspirations 1999 is a compilation of poetry which has been assembled using the work of poets who reside in this are.

The poems vary in style and content, ranging from what they like about their town or city to pleasant memories in life and the joys of the world today.

Each poem is a unique inspiration reflecting on the true emotions from each poetic heart.
A delightful collection for one and all to read time and time again.

Steve Twelvetree
Editor

CONTENTS

The River	Sarah Ferris	1
Daily Loaf	J Gordon	1
What's In A Name?	Eileen Lloyd	2
God's Heritage	I Moss	2
Without	Pamela Sibbering	3
Strike A Light!	Judith Appleby	4
Solitude	Jo Bibby	5
Disharmony	Robert Baslington	6
The Monster From The Deep	Margery Mahon	6
Alcoholic	T Needham	7
Lost Faith	Annie Meighan née Uttley	8
The Rocking Horse	Josephine Moreau	9
War	Dora Doyle	9
Nightwatch	Alan Thomas	10
Ewen McColl's Dirty Old Town	H & L Livesey	11
T'Helm Wind	Rene Roberts	12
For Sale	Colin Kendall	13
Playback	M R Mackinnon-Pattison	14
Problem Solved	Ethel Hutchinson	15
Breakdown	Moyra Summers	16
Man's Folly	David Lamb	16
The Lake	Angela Robinson	17
Good Natured Charlie: Or What Would She Say?	Jack J Docherty	18
Yearning	Lisa Wolfe	19
Duet	Sue Smith	19
The Bookmaker	Robert Burns	20
Dreams	Linda Zulaica	20
Joined-In-Marriage	J Sharples	21
Incapability Brown	Derek Rogerson	22
The Happy Sloven	Sarah Kaye Martin	23
Future Memories	D Lambert	24
Another Sleepless Night	Mark Jones	24
Circles Of Time	Marjorie H Smith	25
The Child I Once Was	Pat Brown	26
Growing Old Together	Rita M Goodwin	26

Title	Author	Page
Up A Tree	Jonathan Cooke	27
Nature's Wrath	D J Holt	28
Winter	Caroline Elizabeth Ashton	29
At The End Of The Day	Julie Gaskell	30
Holiday's End	Marnie Connley	30
On A Downer	Wendy Solari	31
Hydrophobia	Alex J S Marsh	32
Swan Song	Patricia Flynn	33
Rooting Deep	Shaheen Bibi	34
Thoughts On Millennium	Mavis Preston-Riley	35
A Dusty Window	Rose Haycock	35
Bilberry Pie	Brenda Radford	36
Finally	Brian Warne	36
Sanctuary	Richard Wallbank	37
Untitled	Patricia James	37
The Gnome	C Allison	38
Water's Edge	B Pritchard	39
Seasons Come And Go	F Rawlinson	40
The Let Down	Joyce Brown	40
Five Years On	G Mills	41
My Little Secret	Andrea Benita Ross	42
The Seasons Of All Natures	Ian Barton	42
Springtime	Joan Birkby	43
The Endless Conflict	Colin McDonald	44
Ode To Potholes	Gordon Isherwood	45
On The Arrival Of A Yorkshire Terrier Puppy	Rita Roscoe	45
The Crystal Maze?	Neil C Ormesher	46
Lancashire Life	Carol Anne Sheridan	47
Watershed	M Boniface	48
Black Leopard	Jessie Horsley	48
A View Of Nature	Pablo Hamill Magee	49
Lancashire's Lost Nature	David A Chamberlain	50
My Life Of Rings	Edna Cattermole	51
Lucky	David Wright	52
What Next?	M C Cobb	52
Honours - Pre Soccer	Florence Pilkington	53
All Mine	H Cotterill	54

Time	Heather R E Cox	54
My Dreams' Desire	N A Corker	55
Visions	Barbara D Price	56
Arthritis	L Atherton	56
Nightmare	Casey Aitch	57
Witch's Brew	Margaret Parnell	58
Time	J Roberts	58
Sea Moods	Kathleen Gosling	59
What Is Yellow?	Lorraine Dick	60
Calder Vale	Lily Jeffries	60
Not Many Visitors Today	D Taylor	61
School Rules	Kirsty Leighton	61
Mister Snooze	C Creedon	62
Wolf's Message To Man	Hilary Turner	63
The Silence Of Winter	Betsey Prose	64
The Weed	M Goodier	64
Distant Admirer	Martin Howard	65
On Being A Parent	Leila Caryll	66
Escalators	M E Ashley	67
Snobby	B Boertien	68
Millennium Night	Gail Rowan	69
An Industrial Revolution	Pauline Tattersall	70
Cuckoo Land	Jake	71
The Flower Festival	E Kay	72
After The Siege	Stephen Starkie	73
Life In A Caring Community	C Kirkham	74
Local Papers	Brian Humphreys	75
Wild Horses	B Colebourn	76
Rivington Pike	J Morris	76
Castlemaine	Jean Carter	77
Fond Memories Of Old Friends	Ernest Melling	78
My Tiger Cubs	Gareth Wynne Richards	79
The Highfalutin Scotsman	Violet M Corlett	80
Remembrance	Jill Gems	81
Eventide	Eric McBride	82
Lord, I Thank Thee!	M Ross	82
A Poem For Peace	Pauline Mole	83
Alan James	Daisy Cooper	84

Innocent Eyes	Greg King	85
Old Pals	Violet Robinson	86
Sunset	Ruth Waters	86
The 25th December	Kathryn Millington	87
Imagine If Trees Could Talk . . .	Maria Waters	88
The Path Of Life	S Johnson	88
Mothers	Ruby Khan	89
Millennium Hopes	Kathleen Catterall	89
Destruction	L Jones	90
Hausfrau	Janette Harazny	90
Autumn	Angela Pritchard	91
The Reluctant Master	Kathryn Hayward	92
Ethnic Cleansing	Patricia Davis	93
Hubby's Retirement	Joan P Mayer	93
Cross-Country	Holly Stewart	94
Untitled	Nigel Miller	94
A Letter To Sandy From Badger	I Moor	95
A Special Invitation	James Conboy	96
Till Death Us Do Part	Thomas Evason	96
Harvey	Jill Gorman	97
Dear Molly	Margaret Popplewell-Vessey	98
Twice The Fun	Ken Pendlebury	99
The Curse	Chris Longwith	99
A Poem For My Husband	Chérianne Wren	100
Posterity	R Colville	100
Rainbow Of Light	Katherine Kennedy Quaye	101
North West	M Tickle	102
Primrose Gill	Doreen Moscrop	102
Swan	Orry Drinkwater	103
Mixed Feelings	Florence Taylor	104
My Dear Old Dad	Eleanor Dunn	105
Cripple	Kevin Rogers	105
The Village 'Bygone Days'	Nancy Owen	106
A Summer Afternoon	Judi Grayson	107
Metamorphosis	Elsie Gmerek	108
Wondering What Might Have Been	Kim Latham	109

Title	Author	Page
There Is Sadness In My Mind Lord	Catherine Thorburn	109
At Beeston Castle	Nikky Braithwaite	110
Me Dad	J Brooks	111
Choices Of Heart	M Baker	112
Morning On The Fell	Mary Dimond	113
Friendship	Suse Lord	114
The Awakening	John Williams	114
Days	S A Kay	115
In The Dunes	Hans-Henning Nolte	115
Oklahoma Sky	Sylvia Lukeman	116
If Only	Sheila J Drewery	116
Interesting Times . . .? You Must Be Joking	H Stewart	117
The War Party	C Butler	118
Marbury Mill	J Millington	119
Whisperings	Clare Cork	120
Note For Rosie	Tony Tyrer	120
Poets In Repose	John Leighton	121
My Evening Mail	M P John	122
Blue Hour	Michael Collins	122
Death Of A Great	Jaron Hayton	123
Sterile Environment	Kazzie Ingram	124
My Angel	Dawn Graham	125
Lies And Truth	Melvyn Hampson	126
Uniform	Clive Euston	127

THE RIVER

The river rushes up and over stones and lumps of mud,
And hits the bankside with a massive thud.
Rushing through everything in his path,
Anyone walking by gets a little bath.

It's calm now
And floating nicely.
Glinting and gleaming in the sun.
It sparkles like diamonds
Whispering its song
As it goes along
Chattering, gurgling, bubbling away.
All away through the valley
Swirly and whirly on its way
Down to the estuary and into the sea.

Sarah Ferris (10)

DAILY LOAF

The world moves around my loaf of bread
I try to butter it
but it will not stay still long enough
near the equator my butter melts
near the poles it's hard
all the while
going stale
but I keep trying to butter my bread
how frustrating
with a seeming uncontrollable power
it's out of my hands now
oh the pain of missed chances
brought about by greed.

J Gordon

WHAT'S IN A NAME?

You never call me by my name
      Anymore - 'Who am I?'
I say and you, with kindly smile
      Reply 'You're You' and then you sigh,
So deep, impatient, just as once
      You chided me in days gone by.

Your face looks calm. I know this face
      And yet I feel it isn't you.
The eyes see me but when I've gone
      No memory of me will stay - it's true
That I am someone you recall
      From distant past - exactly who?

We do not talk of things that were,
      Of husband, sister or of me.
I try to make you laugh, or sing,
      Remembering how you used to be.
Very houseproud, liked to cook
      Home-made cakes each day for tea.

Contented now no tasks to do.
      Each day for you is just the same.
Your little world is trouble free.
      No thoughts of riches, glamour, fame.
I also do not pine for these,
      Just long for you to say my name.

Eileen Lloyd

GOD'S HERITAGE

No longer able to wander
I do the next best thing
Enjoy viewing the daffodils and primula
Which in the garden come each spring.

So I behold beauty
As Gerard Manley Hopkins wrote,
Maybe the last line of 'trees',
Only God can make a tree bespoke.

I Moss

WITHOUT

Time stood as stone
for four and ten.

The morns, noons
and twilights
bore nothing but
a painful longing for
your presence.

Three score, six and thirty
intangible hours
without you.

Each eve an eternity
without
you to hold.

I had no power to hurry
time's
placid pace . . .

only the will to envisage
your face.

Welcome home.

Pamela Sibbering

STRIKE A LIGHT!

There was a man of great renown
Who used to live in Rammy town.
In a belted raincoat and flat cap
To dress was his usual manner.
His face, so full of character,
Favoured a bulldog chewing a spanner.
So much he looked like Popeye's brother,
Olive Oyl would have been hard pressed
To tell one from the other.

There is a tale told hereabouts,
Of its veracity there may be doubts.
It tells of a journey he undertook
To Bury via Holcombe Brook.

One day he left his stone abode
And headed off down Longsight Road.
Straight as an arrow the way did wend
To the Greenmount fingerpost at the bend,
Where, if further down you look
You might perceive The Old Duke.

At this point, he felt the need
To have a drag on the dreaded weed.
By now the wind had begun to blow
So he turned around to set his pipe aglow.

Around the bowl his hand did cup,
His baccy to inflame.
But instead of looking up
When this deed was done
Instead of turning round again
He went back from where he'd come!

Judith Appleby

SOLITUDE

The wind of change
Rustles in my hair
It seeps through my fingers and toes
Isn't it funny the way the wall grows
The wall once of brambles and thorns
Now has a blooming rose.

To be able to laugh and breathe
The way I choose
Not to be looked upon
In every single move
But in some ways the staring eyes
Do indeed move
In a way that makes it hard to breathe
It blocks my senses in a lot of ways.

My trust is shattered
Paranoid and dazed
Clouds drift in my head
'Once a loser, always a loser'
Someone once said
Maybe I am, maybe I'm not
Only in the eyes of the beholder
My eyes now are fully open
Now that I'm wiser and older.

The dice again is a number six
Full steam ahead and get on with my life
Onwards and outwards, it is now time to live
To live the life I have never once before lived.

Jo Bibby

DISHARMONY

The dark clouds gather over this troubled land,
Despite an understanding and caring hand.
That gave the word, for love, not division,
Yet two communities, treat it with derision.

Protestants and Catholics, Christians the same
Through dogmatism and bigotry, both are to blame
Regardless of the cost they'll force their cause,
May the Christian teaching, show how to pause.

Triumphal Orangemen, parading the street,
The beating drums, and marching of feet.
Nationalists, the marching they won't tolerate,
With such rigidity, comes stalemate.

Religious intolerance, bitterness and hate,
Christians come together, before it is too late.
'Tis Omniscient thought that made your creation,
That all religions be one brotherly nation.

A brotherly nation, together in peace,
Where violence and hatred would finally cease
Through many years, by violence blighted,
End it all now, by love be united.

Robert Baslington

THE MONSTER FROM THE DEEP

Would the monster from the deep weep,
If he knew what he might see if he
Could leave the sea bed?

Can the monster see through the seaweed,
Indeed could he climb aboard a large
Sea horse and ride the waves?

Deep sea caves hold secrets, pearls of
Wisdom, grains of truth, below the roof
Maybe proof of?

Margery Mahon

ALCOHOLIC
(Dedicated to Roy)

My best friend's an alcoholic
He's affected by the drink
It's really took a hold of him
Booze took him to the brink
He always was a drinker
I was once as well
Who will become an alcoholic
Is very hard to tell
He's trying hard to fight it
Knows now that drink's not cool
Drink that was once a pleasure
Now makes him look a fool
It's left him in the gutter
To him drinking's a disease
He just can't stop, when he starts
Till it brings him to his knees
He's trying to confront it
This drink problem he must fight
Take each day as it comes
No drink for him tonight
I'm sure that he can do it
I will help him if I can
For the sake of his sanity
He must become a sober man.

T Needham

LOST FAITH

Our little spark of life, what does it matter?
When we are gone, who will remember us
As the years roll on?
Five decades hence, who will care
What we were or what we did?
No flowers on our tomb, no candles lit in church,
Merely a carved inscription on cold stone.
Only art, literature and music can immortalise our name,
For painting, poetry and melody alone can bring us fame.

The church makes promise of a heaven beyond the grave
Where we shall meet our loved ones gone before.
How can this be? Who can make sense
Of mere human dogma, the product
Of man's imagination, man's desire?
Why? Where? Can such a world exist
And how accommodate humanity deceased?

No! Our life is quickly spent and soon forgotten
As generations come and go.
For time moves on and death draws near
And faith is weakened with each passing year,
Until at last, the moment comes,
Our final breath we draw and all is still,
Is quiet and at peace.
For nothing lasts and nothing at the end will matter,
For the end is *nothing*.

Annie Meighan née Uttley

The Rocking Horse

Remember the rocking horse at the side of the bed,
Waiting for a little curly head.
His brown wooden body and blue velvet saddle,
All set for a little girl to straddle.
It took many weeks for dad to prepare,
As he worked so hard in our attic up there.
And mummy sewed his blanket and seat,
By the light of the gas-lamp flickering weak.
Neddy's black eyes did gaze at the face
Of the child fast asleep, on her pillow.
Beneath the beams of the room in the roof,
As he patiently stood on his rockered hoof.
On that winter's night so long ago,
The flat, dark and silent, slumbered till dawning,
To be aroused with glee and 'Hello Gee-Gee'
On that beautiful Christmas morning.

Josephine Moreau

War

I see something new in this age old world
East and west together everywhere
Intellectuals, adolescents and men of business
Through the spread of war
The world has become one
Is there peace at last
By the wave of a wand?
In the proud cities of the world
I see her people
Deprived, impoverished now
Together searching for power or peace.

Dora Doyle

NIGHTWATCH

His father talks about the Falklands, his grandad spoke about Dunkirk
But he only joined the Army cos he couldn't get no work.
Now he's sitting in a foxhole on the border of Kuwait,
Thinking thoughts of Liverpool and the hour's getting late.
The desert sand blows in his face, the wind is cold and so unkind,
He thinks about his mam and dad and the girl he left behind.
His mam will be dead worried cos he is her only child,
He thinks about his local and a pint of Tetley's mild.

He hears the distant explosions, the jets have dropped another load,
He thinks about that hallowed turf at his beloved Anfield Road.
How long's it going to last, will this madman not give up
In time for him to get home to see Liverpool win the cup.
He looks towards the horizon, the night sky is glowing red,
He thinks about the enemy, some are dying some are dead.
He worries about the battle, and the price he may have to pay,
He thinks about the River Mersey on a cold crisp winter's day.

He cradles his sub-machine gun, like a baby in his arms,
He thinks about his grandma, all her stories, all her charms.
She would tell him about the old days, when front doors were left ajar
And the summer sun was so hot that it melted all the tar.
Alaleo and kick the can and ollies in the gutter,
And dripping on the bread cos there wasn't any butter.
He shifts his position slightly because he's cramped and he is cold,
He still loves his grandma's stories although he's nineteen years old.
His young life has been interrupted by a dictator's evil plan,
And maybe on the morrow, this young boy becomes a man.

His nightwatch is almost over, another chapter in his story,
The desert day is dawning, and he marvels at its glory.
The sun is an orange fire, that warms him to the bone,
As he strides back to his bivouac, we must remember he's not alone,
For all our hopes and prayers go with him, to guide him through
                                                       this hell
May God put his arms around him, and bring him back home
                                                      safe and well.

Alan Thomas

EWEN MCCOLL'S DIRTY OLD TOWN

Only one song,
        I've heard of my home.
It tells of a town,
        Dirty and old.
But of people with heritage,
        Proud, bold.
A great axe taken,
        To chop it down.
   Slums taken from eyesight.
Cotton mills died.
          From their might.
Now to see SALFORD,
        In a new light.
   Clean air, skies of bright.
So Jimmy Miller,
        Your song's still heard.
        But Salford had to evolve.
Though All its problems
        haven't been solved.
Jimmy Miller, famous you never became.
But Ewen McColl did,
        You being, the very same.

H & L Livesey

T'HELM WIND

When the helm wind doth blow - you'll jolly soon know
When to get out your ganzie and vest.
No time for silk socks, for your feet feel like rocks
And you'll find out that t'fireside's best.

We'll either get snow - or fog on the go,
Or rain coming down - in great lashings.
Lambs cling to their mudders, cows shudder their udders
It's no time to have naked passions.

It gets dark about four, and you're glad the day's o'er
Just see what's on't telly tonight.
And then when you're sitting and start your knitting
The 'Grid' fails and out goes the light.

You feel for a candle - get hold of a handle -
Of the teapot, which hasn't been emptied.
It spills on the floor - you can't stand any more.
You swear like a trooper when tempted,

So you get into bed - it's bedsocks instead
Of wearing a whiff of Chanel.
A night-cap like Noddy - a steaming hot toddy
A chest soothed with Vic rub as well.

The helm's still roaring - the rain's still pouring
Tomorrow will be just the same.
When resident in Eden - it's no good receding
The weather is part of the game.

Don't long for a hero, if the weather's sub-zero,
Don't wish for a fantasy's roam.
Go out for a booze-up? No, just get your shoes off!
When t'helm's on - there's no place like
Home.

Rene Roberts

For Sale

There's a house in my head which has five rooms
That once echoed to the sound of amplified thoughts.
Though a few sticks of furniture still remain,
The inhabitants have long since become adult and absent
And their window frames rot in the shadows of disuse.

I burned the fingers of innocence
One night beneath trees long ago.

I dressed my ambitions in dignity
But they have left home,
Wearing what once belonged to me.

My passion was currency
Which I spent on a girl
Who is a stranger to me now.
I am penniless.

I always fought for my honesty
But the discovery of people more honest than myself
Led me to believe that I was less than honest.
I overpriced my honesty
And sold it to the nearest fool.

Integrity remained a while longer
Battle scarred and clinging on
But little use on its own.
The day it died, I cut up my integrity
Like an out-of-date credit card
And threw it down for the birds.

Now this house is in darkness
And soon the estate agent of my life
Will move in to erect the 'For Sale' signs
And I will be sold
To a much bigger concern.

Colin Kendall

Playback

Roam again these heathered hills
        Fills the thoughts a youngster made
Feel the rain-drenched bracken
        Whackin' round the knees
Breathe the pine tree filtered air
        Where in younger days we played
See rowan trees that stand aloft
        Softly moving in the breeze
Over grey rocks lithely trekked
        Flecked with thick green moss
Spruce trees scented by the sun
        Run with drops of fresh fall rain
Harebells in the stubby grass
        Pass where gorses' spikes can toss
Ice-cold water from the streams
        Creams the parched throat again
Raise a grouse in fluttered fear
        Hear the pee-wit's painful cry
Climb the oak tree and the ash
        Splash the naked swimming mime
Trout stream fishing pin and thread
        Tread the marsh and mud nearby
Run the gauntlet through the corn
        Scorn the world of metered time
Ambitions coloured ideals flick
        Quick change with easy glossy page
Tomorrow's world is far away
        Pay no heed to future's wants
Wrap the problems in your dreams
        Streams your border, trees your cage

Heathered hills and meadows green
        Screen of distance childhood haunts
Country boots these pathways trod -
        Now my feel are city shod.

M R Mackinnon-Pattison

PROBLEM SOLVED

Settled down in high glee,
To watch the TV.
With a packet of crisps,
And a nice cup of tea.

Looking forward with delight
To a long awaited pleasure,
Went out like a light,
Missed the programme altogether.

When I opened my eyes
That vintage film had gone.
The credits were rolling,
'The End' had just come.

In future, when I'm tired,
I'll have a bit of sense,
Buying a video recorder
Is well worth the expense.

When I can organise
My evening's recreation.
If I miss some, I'll use re-wind,
A much happier situation.

Ethel Hutchinson

BREAKDOWN

When there is
No signpost
No landmark
When the world is dark
And the terrain
Unfamiliar
When there is no one to beckon
And no voice to whisper
No sound
Only self
And the long shadow of
Time
Ever behind
When at last there is nothing
Of substance to
Remind of
Who you are
How then
To find
The tiny light
Somewhere to shine
The way home.

Moyra Summers

MAN'S FOLLY

The moons of endor glowing before ye,
The sun's heat scorching the flesh of the innocents,
The mists putrefying the air, once clean,
Maybe one day you mortals may see your folly, until now unseen,

Rising oceans, deadly snakes,
Fallen cities, mortals' mistakes,
Poisoned vipers, demons, snipers,
Angels cry, as their children die,

Can you see the lanterns glowing on the end of the dragon's tail?
If not reached then destiny shall surely prevail,
Blood shall run thicker than lava from below,
Make your decision,
Up above, or down below!

David Lamb

THE LAKE

When my thoughts were sad and sore
I'd wander down to Ullswater shore.
There I'd watch the changing scene
and come away feeling quite serene.

The hills and valleys round about
would echo to my brother's shout.
As the sparkling ripples met the shore
I could see my parents content once more.

Even when the water looked rough and black,
beneath the clouds there was always a crack
showing a light behind the hills
bringing hope that could cure all ills.

I've sailed on the Lady of the Lake
with sun sparkled diamonds in her wake.
There I've paddled a blow-up boat - and
walking with the strength of my husband's hand.

Laughter has outweighed the tears,
Love has taken away the fears.
Clouds and darkness are replaced by the sun
at Ullswater Lake, my favourite one.

Angela Robinson

GOOD NATURED CHARLIE: OR WHAT WOULD SHE SAY?

What is that vision I see there before me?
The way she moves is so delightful to see!
What would she say if I walked over to parley?
Would I be just another good-natured Charlie?

I've just got to go over and take a chance
It's a night of magic and a night of romance.
'Hello lovely lady with a sparkle in your eyes
Would you like your life to have a happy surprise?'

'Let's go downstairs to the dancing floor
Where we can do the polka and maybe more!
Though I love to see you do the cancan!
Why not dance with the man that I am?'

'Dancing with you is such a joy
Though I know I'm not your only boy.
So please don't answer me in a rage
Please dance for me on the music hall stage.'

'Oh Penny, now that I know your lovely name
I want to give you a chance of sweet fame!
No longer dancing high on the hot gin bar
For a lady like you will become a star!'

'Oh Penny, Delightful I know you'll be true
There's nothing in the world I wouldn't do for you
Just to see you sing and dance on the stage of life
Would be like being a perfect husband and wife.'

'Oh Penny, Delightful is her name
I gave her a chance, and she took it of fame!
The Queen of the music hall now she is
From gin served hot
To Champagne fizz!'

Jack J Docherty

YEARNING

I've now been on my own for five long years
I loved my husband dearly, love him still.
But being human, I long for someone dear
To hold me, kiss me and my life to fill.

There is someone I like and he likes me
But both of us are set in our ways.
Have families of whom we are not free
And if, with common ground, a future we could face.

We meet within a group, cocooned by our friends
As yet we have not been alone, but feel the flow
Of warmth between us, an affinity I sense
Which gives me hope as our friendship grows.

Lisa Wolfe

DUET

Intro - strings taut and finely tuned
Trembling fingers caress them.
Teasing sweet music, piano, pianissimo.
The rhythm is established
A beat emerges, answered by playful melody.
They soar together, reaching heights
beyond imagination.
Allegro and sforzando
Passion roused fortissimo.
A raging climax -
No variation on a theme,
Just gentle pizzicato, echoing a heartbeat.
Players and instruments resting for an encore.

Sue Smith

THE BOOKMAKER

A lot of racing
Is animal roulette
You pick a number
Hoping to collect.

The obvious choice
On known form
Seldom succeeds
That is the norm.

The bookies ploy
Hoping others follow
Their wily ways
Leave the rest in sorrow.

They often insist
On things their way
And you unlikely
To have much sway.

Robert Burns

DREAMS

The dreams I have
Should all be burnt
For all they bring
Is harm;
But patiently,
And with such care,
I gently
Them embalm.

Linda Zulaica

JOINED-IN-MARRIAGE

Today as you both wake up to a brand new beginning on your
                                                                  Wedding Day,
There'll be help, advice and support to guide you on your way.
Also plenty of decisions, commitments and confessions, you will make.
As you declare all inner love in the vows you will certainly take:
All friends and family (the congregation) are waiting very anxiously
                                                                            in church,
Knowing very well that the groom will not be left in the lurch.
The organ starts playing the Bridal Walk as she is finally here,
The groom looks lovingly on the girl so radiant and whom he
                                                                           holds dear:
The bell's ring out as two single people in love are joined as one,
The old world has ended and a new start has just begun.
Each moment will always be treasured throughout all your married life,
Your devotion and loyalty to each other is eternal now - you're man
                                                                          and wife:
On your honeymoon you shall travel to a destination you're sure to go,
Getting to spend this special night and each other in privacy - you
                                                                           will know,
As each anniversary comes, all of the day will be remembered -
                                                                    extremely well,
As being just perfect and so right, also absolutely swell:
Next is buying a place that is new and somewhere to call home,
Filling it with mementoes and fittings and making it your palace dome,
In years to come there will probably be the warmness of a boy -
                                                                      or girl child.
Keeping you busy, on your toes, but oh so lovely, free and wild:

J Sharples

INCAPABILITY BROWN

The world as usual spins on by
while he lolls idle wondering why
the fates refuse to smile his way.
Perhaps they will! - Another day.

Now on that side I'll plant a tree.
Close by the lily pond will be
a mass of colour; scents and shade.
Tomorrow - when I find that spade.

A kitchen garden over there,
with apple, plum and peach and pear
trees, bearing fruit will grow -
I'll borrow Uncle William's hoe.

A rustic bower festooned with roses.
I have it! Now if one supposes
an oval ornamental lake -
I wonder where one buys a rake?

Ah! But sloth is bliss and toil is sorrow.
I'll rest today and work tomorrow.
This hour is meant to doze and dream,
Why mar a moment so serene
with thoughts of labour spoil my play.
Best leave it for another day.

The season's wrong, the hour grows late.
I'd scarcely start - I know, I'll wait
until another spring is nigh -
'til then I'll sit, and dream, and sigh!

Derek Rogerson

THE HAPPY SLOVEN

I'm not harassed by any one individual
I'm thoroughly harassed by life
Revealing my flaws as the perfect mother
Flaunting my inadequacies as the ideal wife
Images of smiling content maternal ones
Seem to greet me at every turn
Am I alone in hating 12 piece jigsaws
And cutesy videos that make me squirm?
I view muddy children as happy ones
Girls can't play properly in a dress
They'll clean, and as we know from the soap ads
Whiter whites, happy mum, equals no stress
And as for the ideal wife palaver
That's even harder because I'm not wed
As near as damn it but not legally
Though for fourteen years we've shared a bed
On the housewife front at hurdle one I stumble
As a home-maker I'm a bit of a joke
I can think of better things than wiping skirtings
I just don't share the enthusiasm of other folk
I can't muster interest in new cleaning products
Advertisement executives would reel in shock
It's my mess and right now it's not bothering
If it's going to offend, I suggest you don't knock
We're all happy, healthy, clean and contented
Get plenty of love, laughter, fun and fresh air
So go harass some other self-doubting poor soul
'Cos I've just realised, though not perfect, I don't care.

Sarah Kaye Martin

FUTURE MEMORIES

Neat and tidy
To the boundary
The stones in rows
Each mark a memory.

Despite the golden
Moments past,
They turn to dust
Or turn to ash.

Some are blessed with pretty flowers.
Laid with care
To help them dare
To while away Eternity's hours.

But the layers will be laid,
Down besides them in the grave.
Then together 'neath the blades,
There forever will they fade.

D Lambert

ANOTHER SLEEPLESS NIGHT

Tuesday 3.30am,
It's happened once again.
Taken aback by a sting in the tale,
From a beautiful face,
Soft, white and pale.

No name, no number, no contact address,
Just your memory turned into a mess;
Your mind can't think nor concentrate,
It's just left with time to contemplate.

Can't lose her, can't shake her,
Or get her out of your head.
You'll lie there all night,
Pondering in bed.

Outside you can hear the pouring of rain,
While the alarm clock reminds you,
It's 3.30am.

Mark Jones

CIRCLES OF TIME

The circles of our life begin
From our first day on Earth,
With those around to love us
Our first few years from birth.

Then schooldays come and friends we make
We treasure each new day,
When cares are few, sorrows unknown
We go our happy way.

We're growing up and at that time
Our circle tightens round,
We find in life more challenges
By duties we are bound.

Then comes the final circle
As age its toll doth take.
Yet on and on, and round and round
We hope our worth to make.

The circle of life goes on and on,
Two thousand years now past,
We pray the circle still revolves
And peace may reign at last.

Marjorie H Smith

THE CHILD I ONCE WAS

When I was a child
I thought the world could be mine
That I could just reach out and take a little piece
But I was looking at the world
Through the eyes of a child
Innocent and naive.

The child in me has long gone
The innocence lost forever
So I close my eyes and try to imagine
The child I once was
The child that was lost
But in my mind's eye
I can no longer see she
I can only see me . . .
The woman who will miss her
                        For ever.

Pat Brown

GROWING OLD TOGETHER

As time rolls by, contentment grows,
And our once young love matures.

Our happiness means sharing
Our happiness means caring.
The little things we do and say
To help each other day by day.

The family we have reared together
Have made us oh so proud.
It wasn't easy all the time,
Many difficult passages in our prime.

But God grant us more time together
To live and love now at our leisure.
Our grandchildren to fully enjoy
And hopefully see them grow by.

Togetherness - sharing so much pleasure,
Into old age, a life story to treasure.

Rita M Goodwin

UP A TREE

When early autumn's just arrived
Some of the plants have not survived
The air is cool and very nice
In the morning it's as cold as ice.

The birds that sing in the open air
I like to find and I like to stare
All the year the world is sweet
So step outside it's like a treat.

There's wild life all around the Earth
I couldn't think how much it's worth
It's so exciting if you look
It's so much better than a book.

So why don't you come outside more
Just get some shoes and open the door
I am telling you now, it's really good
So please come out you really should.

This is something you should try
So please think twice I've told you why
Run around, climb a tree
If you do this - you're like me.

Jonathan Cooke (9)

NATURE'S WRATH

A rod of lightning split the sky
And thunder rumbled far away.
Inky clouds began to fly
Like demons sweeping up the bay.
Rumbles now became a roar
Webs of flickering light appear,
With spears descending from its core
Burned and ravished the wooden pier
Wall of wind raged from the sea,
Swamped the cliffs came ever near
To claim the land, all the lea
The sheep had grazed for many a year.
The mighty fist of wroth advanced,
Nature as its engineer.
With vicious force it rips asunder
All the outcrop that is near.
Devouring all within its sight
So deafening to the naked ear.
Wonder of wonders what a sight
Filling all with awe and fear.
At last the thundering waves are ebbing
Stormy winds have dropped a gear,
Terrain is getting back to normal
Wounded cliffs do soon appear
Bandaged in a cloak of sunshine,
Scars will last for many a year.
All is quiet, in the meantime
Calming water laugh and leer,
As if to say this, my kingdom.
Nothing now I have to fear.

D J Holt

WINTER

It is June 13th
A summer day outside
And yet winter rules my spirit.

I feel his death upon me,
Putting coldness in my heart,
Shivers down my spine,
And ice into my soul.
What could have been is now no more.

Yet still from far away and long ago,
Summer memories together breathe
Their fiery breath into me,
Recalling passions lost
And make me live again.

Grief retreating as dreams come
But only at night, enwrapped in Morpheus' arms,
I dream of ardent fires melting
Ice into warm pools
The laughter and smiles appear once more.

Awakening from slumber
The bitter memories return.
They make me ache,
And wish for winter's easy coolness
To freeze me once again.

Caroline Elizabeth Ashton

At The End Of The Day

Heavenly Father.
  The day is drawing to a close,
  and I am weary, my heart is heavy
  my mind so troubled.
  Yet I know Your love will never fail me.
  I know what those unseen hands of love
  did for 'me'. When once before I was 'too
  tired' or 'too ill' to care for myself.
  So great was my faith that I was 'unafraid'
  to open up my heart, to open up my mind
  to open up my soul unto You, thus allowing
  the creative force to enter in.
  Once again I come before You,
  infuse me with Your love
  give me the richness of the tapestry.
  Let me gather up that thin gold thread
  and weave it into my whole being,
  and draw me on to Your wonderful pathway
  of truth and enlightenment
  that I may leave it 'never'.

Julie Gaskell

Holiday's End

(When I was seven)

They're going home
I don't want to go.
I've had such fun,
Holidaying - you know.

The grown-ups don't mind
There's things to be done -
Back to the grind
The holiday week's gone.

The ferry boat is awaiting,
Soon to be on the sail
to home. A very long way.
From a holiday remembered
Still to this very day.

Marnie Connley

ON A DOWNER

Life, so confusing, which way should I turn?
So many mistakes have I made, will I ever learn?
Happiness, will that ever be me?
A soulmate to find, but a part still free.
A bond without words is what I seek,
Does a man exist to whom my heart will speak?

To family and friends my personality must change,
They say I must show anger, that to me will be strange.
I try to live my life without hurting a soul,
Treat others how I wish to be treated, this is my role.
A 'doormat' is what everyone seems to say
But at the end of the day, it is I who must pay.

Loneliness, a feeling very few understand,
Wandering alone through a storm of sand,
Seek and Ye shall find, but where is the map?
My self-worth eroding, water dripping from a tap.
Who am I? What should I do and where should I go?
Instinct, run away, only my two cats would know.

So many questions, my mind seems to ask,
Life always an act, my face an illusion, a mask.
If I knew the problem , I could be absolved of the blame,
No matter which words, I still feel the same,
Tears, my only outlet, damp lines on my face,
How do I escape from my head and out of the rat race?

Wendy Solari

HYDROPHOBIA

room   hot
coffee   pot
you   cold
me   bold

drink   brandy
you   randy
lips   pout
lights   out

warm   bed
night   fled
love   given
past   forgiven

dawn   broken
goodbye   spoken
train   gone
me   alone

walking in the dark, where no songs are
where dead birds stare through running, dragging waves
and seaweed tangles the pebbles and driftwood

gone to your island
me without a boat
and afraid of those waters

Alex J S Marsh

Swan Song

Walking by the water
We came across magical swans
Tending their young
Weeks and weeks of waiting
Patiently sitting
Comes the day
The young ones are born
So tiny, so delicate
White wisps of down
So quiet, so beautiful
Never a sound

The world is fraught with danger
Time to move on
No rushing, no frightening their young
Quietly, in orderly fashion, one by one
No pecking, no pushing -
Down to the water's edge
The little flock descends

Mother swan, first in the water
With grace - she waits
First one little one
Delicately hops in
The others soon follow
Like feathers in the wind
Father fluffs his chest - he waits
Takes to the water
Last baby follows him

Stately procession moves on
Quietly, silently
The danger is gone.

Patricia Flynn

ROOTING DEEP

Searching for our roots is how this began.
Finding the era our parents longed for once again.
Caring honest and righteous people
relations who longed to meet us.
A return journey by plane
the start of our long distant search.
Some say the greatest wonder of the sky
on board we agree a missile waiting to launch.
Journey ends with an array of sunlight and a halt.
Overwhelmed we stood under the giant wonder of the sky,
breath by breath inhaling dry warm air of our parents birthplace.
There we met those caring righteous and honest people
relations waiting to meet us.
Rooting deep we fell into a maze.
Towards every corner we ran to no avail.
Patience is a virtue comforted our minds.
A relation, blood caring and righteous we shall find.
Many close of blood we met along the trail
our child within confided for help against the evil and failed.
As waves of close blood crashed around the maze
the vulnerable child our innocence began drowning under an evil veil.
Our minds, hearts and souls feeling suicidal.
Then a shadow from above their came
the greatest wonder of the sky boarded us in
Like a missile it launched
With a cloud of showers it came to a halt
stood overwhelmed under the giant of the sky
breath by breath inhaling the musty damp air of our birthplace
Safely locked in a blackmail of emotions
we await our return to the maze and our relations.

Shaheen Bibi

THOUGHTS ON MILLENNIUM

It's two thousand years, since we started to count.
Such achievements made, to what do they amount.
From pole to pole, and east to west, man plunges the depths
                                              and climbs Everest.
Man can traverse the planets, as far as can be,
Quickly explore, and be home for tea.
Communicate via a satellite dish
E-mail a message to the moon, if you wish.
Anything can happen in this wide world of Earth.
Everything discovered, and, what is it worth?
Knowledge we have gained, some skills we have lost,
Are people still winning and what is the cost?

Mavis Preston-Riley

A DUSTY WINDOW

In between particles of dust
Are bits of feelings.
Feelings that drift,
Floating in time.
Glistening by moonlight,
Snowing on surfaces,
Skating across windows,
Circling in emptiness.
Some leave my room,
Stopping who knows where?
Fields, oceans, clouds.
Enveloping feelings.
Circling dust.

Rose Haycock

BILBERRY PIE

On warm summer days the pickers go,
To Kemple End where the bilberries grow.
Filling their polythene bags to the top.
They look like bees round a honey pot.

They sweat and toil in the summer air,
Stripping the bilberry bushes bare,
Then with fingers all stained and aching backs
They decide to rest and eat their snacks.

They drink their coffee and sit and chat,
Look at the view and marvel at that.
They rest for a while, breathe in the good air,
Then off home they go the pie to prepare.

When all is ready and the tea table set
They cannot wait at the pie to get,
For they know the frozen food they can buy
Will never compare with the fresh bilberry pie.

Brenda Radford

FINALLY

I've got to put something to bed,
Once and for all, finally, rendered dead.
I need to let go, shake it out of my hair.
How do you let go, when you still can't help but care?
But when all's been said, and all's been done,
Do I wash my hands, and decide to run?
Do I stop to care, do I stop to think?
Do I stop, with my head in my hands, unable to blink?
Now the tears have started stinging, a punishment for the pain.
The pain received for putting it to bed, again, and again, and again.

Brian Warne

SANCTUARY

Like an all encompassing cloak
the dark night covers all
save for the winking of a lonely star
shining through a hole in heaven.

The breath from an angel's mouth
gently caresses my frozen cheek
returning some warmth to my life
to the distant beating of my heart.

Slowly my aching limbs move onward
crunching the cinders below my feet
carrying me onward through the night
looking for a distant light I know is there.

Through frost-encrusted eyelids I see
through the haze of a winter's night
the ascending smoke of a distant lodge
the pilgrim is home at last.

Richard Wallbank

UNTITLED

I feel like a summer leaf that he been torn off an autumn tree.
Unwillingly blown and carried relentlessly downwards,
slowly to the ground below.
Upon seeing a mountain of solid leaves beneath,
the decomposing, rotting compost to which my grave awaits.
My needs are inside one of those three dimensional pictures,
that you need to patiently stare and
await for the shape of the intended picture to appear.
Is there anyone, with the love and patience to wait for me.

Patricia James

The Gnome

I walked into a garden
And there upon a stone
I saw a small man sitting
Just like a garden gnome.
Imagine my surprise,
When he, a twinkle in his eye,
Said, 'Morning sir, who may you be?'
To which I did reply,
'I'm here to see this garden
I'm told it's very rare
It's overgrown with weeds and such
It could do with some care.'
He smiled and winked
And then he said, 'You're just the very man.
If you could clean this garden up
You look as if you can,
And when you're through, I'll grant a wish
To pay for all your time.'
So spade in hand, I set to work
And laboured until nine.
It took till dusk to finish it
But when it all was done
I asked about the wish
To which, he answered, 'Son
What age are you?'
And I replied, 'I'm thirty five years old.'
'And you still believe in fairies then
Well, well, bless my soul!'

C Allison

WATER'S EDGE

Through the mist I saw him at the water's edge,
its wash lapping at his feet.
He stood unmoving,
giving no indication of life,
just a dark shadow whose features never met mine.
Then, the mist thickened,
it surrounded his shape.

He was taken by the mist,
sunken into it,
floating, drifting away, or upwards
till he was no longer in my eye.
Had I witnessed a trick of the eye?
Or was it self delusion.
I questioned my sanity at this lost apparition,
this unreality.

Then, as the sun broke through the mist
into fingers of light,
something caught my eye
as the sun struck to make it glint.
Nestled between the pebbled washed edges,
it lay shining.
My fingers searched the mist into the water,
reaching out I clutched it firmly
bringing it to my eyes.
It was a band of gold, a wedding ring.

B Pritchard

Seasons Come And Go

Winter's elements of wind and rain
Pitter-pat against the windowpane.
The inclement mantle of frost and snow
Whilst we stay snug and warm by the fireside glow.

What comfort to nestle by a burning log!
The hearth surrounded by a sleeping dog.
As sun imposes upon a dark tilth floor
Then nature tentatively opens up her pantry door.

Seedlings burst upon us, now it's springtime
To nature's full fruition in such a temperate clime.
Swaying blooms bedeck the flower beds
Of gnarled hands at work in potting sheds.
Ericas, brooms, foliage and shrubs
A green tapestry spangled with unfurled buds.

The mighty trees with their leaf-tree spread
Reincarnation the Almighty said.
Autumn green, red, and yellow hues
Time to discard the muddy garden shoes
The cloak of winter brings to a head
All summer's flourished turned to dead.

F Rawlinson

The Let Down

Couldn't wait to tell them
My exciting news,
A poem to be published,
Me - a modern muse!

All day long I savoured
The thought of their delight,
Their joy in my achievement,
My star would shine so bright!

Six o'clock, they're home at last,
The atmosphere felt heady,
Bursting with pride, I told them,
'Oh' they said, 'Is tea ready?'

Joyce Brown

FIVE YEARS ON

Is it not high time that I got some sleep
and cast this load from my mind?
I'm still waiting for the magic relief
they told me would come with time.

Time, tick-tock, the healer of pain
said they, would make it disappear,
but a force this strong is a stubborn stain,
immobile, resolute, without fear.

My minutes are stolen, my middays clocked,
it won't be eternal, said they;
just stick it out, all will pass
and you'll be glad you did - one day.

But the minutes crawl, the hours won't budge
and your face crystal clear, still lingers.
They were wrong, say I, time-warp style,
stuck here, this thread round your finger.

So sleep I cannot, nor rest will I get
until your memory is faded and gone
with the wind and my ashes we'll blow away,
and naught but our names will live on . . .

G Mills

MY LITTLE SECRET

I don't have much
Just one little pleasure.
It's a little bit naughty
But it's something I treasure.
I wait until night
When I'm all alone.
I lock the doors
And won't answer the phone.
I can't resist my naughty secret.
I don't want to share it,
It's mine and I'll keep it.
I curl up my feet
And then open the box.
My secret treasure,
My Milk Tray chocs.

Andrea Benita Ross

THE SEASONS OF ALL NATURES

Moods are like the weather, changeable.
Passions are like the wind speed, variable.
High pressure, followed by depressions
Thoughts gathering clouds, climatic changes
Leading to dangerous undercurrents
Apocalyptic visions of the end of the world.

The seasons are like our natures, unpredictable,
Charts show cyclones, whirlwinds and hurricanes
Outlook unstable,
Drifting thought clouds with no direction,
A storm in a teacup
A kitchen filled with thunder.

Behaviour patterns, like weather patterns,
Are a patchwork quilt.
If our tempers unravel
We can blame it on the rain,
Moods are like the wind speeds, variable.
Our true natures are seasoned by our thoughts.

Ian Barton

SPRINGTIME

Hawthorn blossoms on the bough,
Make Maytime hedgerows glow,
It seems like Mother Nature,
Has sprinkled them with snow.

The verdant verges come alive,
With many varied hue,
As bluebells and forget-me-nots
Give out a hint of blue.

The oak, the ash, the chestnut,
The elm and elder too,
Wake up each spring to show the world,
Their buds, as if on cue.

As dandelions and buttercups
Turn fields to cloth of gold,
The sparrows in their hidden nests
Make quarrels loud and bold.

The sweet sounds of the songbird's trill,
As they hover on the wing,
Oh yes! It is a wondrous place
Is England in the spring.

Joan Birkby

THE ENDLESS CONFLICT

There is a spirit in all of us trying to reach the light,
but the spirit is uneasy as we see
us humans pushing, shoving and wanting to fight.

Searching for materialism and status at any cost,
confronting the ego while the spirit gets lost.
What will be the final price
when the ego is fed and everything on the outside
looks so pretty and nice.

The ego tells us to tramp and tread
on anybody or anything as long as it get fed,
but what a price the spirit has to pay as we toss and
turn and sweat and cry as we lie each night in bed.

We make a promise never again,
but with the new day we continue to give the sprit new pain.
Life's rushing by and the ego has only one thought,
grab everybody and everything that can be bought.

Oh my spirit, I know you want what is right
please strengthen me to stop this fight
between the ego and you.
As I know lovely spirit that all I need do,
is unto myself, just be true.

Colin McDonald

Ode To Potholes

Potholes, potholes everywhere with not a place to go,
The asphalt gang they come and go - then there's another so and so,
The holes, they come by day and night, they stealthily appear,
Pedestrians tripping here and there, m'thinks they've been on t' beer,
But no, it's t'holes, some big some small,
Some as big as the Albert Hall.
Some really deep called 'Super Hole',
Some, in fact, producing coal.
Towns take part in competitions
For t' deepest holes in t' best positions,
They submit holes in various sizes,
And t' residual body awards the prizes,
Some day the roads will be relaid,
And pavements properly repaved
When rockets travel to the moon
(resurfacing can't come too soon)
But until then we're under tension,
Steady lad, watch t' cars suspension.

Gordon Isherwood

On The Arrival Of A Yorkshire Terrier Puppy

A warm dumpling of soft fur.
Two sharp brown eyes, a mischievous air.
An appealing face, a delicious yawn.
·A sweet expression, melting hearts of stone.
Full of feminine wiles and inquisitive seeking.
A destructive spoiler of papers we're keeping.
Yet no matter how badly Saffron behaves,
With a whimsical glance - she captures her slaves.

Rita Roscoe

THE CRYSTAL MAZE?

Wrapped within the metallic skin.
Reflecting sunlight and life akin.
Rotating crystals, refracting light,
Life's changing colours set eyes abright!

As circumstance set man's wheel whirring
Gripping hands get patterns turns.
Rainbow's colours and many more,
Spectrum of our joys and woe?

Twisting, sliding, the tinctured rays
Guides us through our shifting days.
In symmetry perfect, designs do dance
Here the mirror is real romance!

Schemata move with edgy grace,
Mimics us, and man's rat race.
Myriad forms and permutations,
Echo mortals' combinations?

The shapes are many, seems no conclusion!
As lifetime's alleys, complete confusion!
But soon enough the cycle's finished
As our lifetime is diminished

This cyclic passage of glass and hue
A parallel of me and you?
But without lamp, or light from skies,
Just like us: the image dies.

Neil C Ormesher

LANCASHIRE LIFE

It's cold, smutty and grey,
The little boys sent out to play.
Cobbled streets live galore,
Terraced houses row by row.

Round the gas lamps meet
Shabbily dressed kids to greet.
Clogs spark the mucky street,
Jumping the trams for a treat.

The mother blackens the grate,
She's been to the shop for food on the slate.
Her husband's been laid off,
Alas again there is no dosh.

Hungry children at her heels,
Cry, pleading for a meal.
Hard times are here again,
Alas another one's on the way.

Hardship, poverty, full of gloom,
Again and again the same old tune.
His backie tin's nowt in,
The pawn shops full to the brim.

Bedtime comes once again,
Share a crust to ease the pain.
Overcoats cover the tattered beds,
Into the dampen parlour tread.

Head to toe they lie
Nit and fleas have a fight.
Mother and dad soon join the kids
Another night of poverty bliss.

Carol Anne Sheridan

WATERSHED

Water flowing, ever going to find
its own
level.

Rushing, gushing forth - an earth force
It flows
again

Life provider, life eraser.
Who will
decide?

Water moving, always soothing.
Lulls all
senses.

It will cleanse me, when I feel the
need to
revive.

Balm and blessing, all replenishing
water of
life.

M Boniface

BLACK LEOPARD

Leopard black as darkest night
Eyes like two green jewels set
Graceful, pleasing, to the sight
Spots concealed 'Neath coat of jet.

Indolently draped along the branch
Hidden from below, he hides concealed
Waiting for a creature who by chance
Should venture 'near his hide of leafy green.

Dropping lithely from the tree
Such strategy can hardly fail
With tooth and claw he fights so savagely
His victim's struggles are to no avail.

What tragic twist of fate it be
That nature's ruling must apply
The evidence is plain to see
If one must live, then another must die.

Jessie Horsley

A VIEW OF NATURE

Stop, look and listen
    Take in a breath of fresh air,
Slow down, absorb the things of nature,
    It's absolutely everywhere.
Birds fly high and low,
    Smell the aroma of various flowers see how they grow.
Observe the trees and vegetation,
    The beautiful light that is cast upon it.
Sun by day . . . silvery moon during night.
Butterflies flutter without sound . . .
    Bees explore flowers -
As insects crawl over and beneath the ground.
The different seasons come,
    Leaving each their own impression.
Animals hibernate at their own discretion.
The beauty is there for all to see . . .
    So think you people who are missing
Take in a long deep breath of fresh air
    And *stop - look -* and *listen!*

Pablo Hamill Magee

LANCASHIRE'S LOST NATURE

Percy the pet peacock escapes from the hill farm
And, perched on a wall,
Lonely calls across the Rossendale Valley for a mate to charm.

Meanwhile, a heron flies westbound along the M62
But the commuters who notice are few.

Above a traffic island,
Lapwings clumsily tumble through the sky crying 'peewit'.

In Blackburn there's a spaniel who tries to follow the scent
Of the rush-hour traffic
But the canned drivers just honk their horns at it.

A kestrel hovers above the verge
To spy the drowned-out screeching shrew.

Rabbits in burrows
Twitch their noses at the ozone smog.

An albino frog is splashed across the headlines
Of a local rag.

Badgers are ripped to pieces
By baiters who brag.

The bee swells pollen sacks
On GM rapeseed.

Rooks and crows flock to mock
The last skylark to disappear into a song over the Bowland Fell.

The red squirrel is pushed away by the grey
Trout are prey to sex-changing PCB's in the River Irwell.

The furtive fox survives on discarded fast food.
The a Burnley barn owl suffers a rude awakening
To a luxury conversion of its home.

Under the cover of darkness,
Carcasses of fat rats
Are flushed out to sea under Blackpool Pier.

David A Chamberlain

MY LIFE OF RINGS

My life revolved around a ring - my first 'a ring of roses'
January being my birth date - snowdrops - my bunch of posies.

Next a special friendship ring - made of black elephant hair
Banded by two golden clasps - made he and I a special pair.

Soon came my lovely engagement ring - in its beautiful plush lined box.
Our love was strengthened daily - I felt like Cinderella, my prince with
                                                              just one sock.

At Xmas time - yet another ring - I loved him so much dearer
A blood-red garnet - my birthstone held - heart beating - knowing
                                                      my wedding day nearer.

Father time moves on - and six sons our marriage bless -
Where has time flown - now my eternity ring I guess.

Relations send us gifts of silver - yet one good friend a silver ring
Enclosed in its oval casing - blue butterfly - bright as the spring.

Now I am so sorry to say - we never reached our golden day
The reaper came and took my love - now a wait to join him up above.

Though gnarled with age and growing old.
Yet I still wear with pride, my ring of gold

Edna Cattermole

LUCKY

I've never had a kitten before.
I've called him 'Lucky'.

He's black and white
With a stripe down his back
And he purrs like a motorbike
On the Belle Vue track.

He spends all his days:
    eating, drinking and sleeping
    playing, hiding and peeping.

    Dancing at shadows, scratching at chairs,
    turning somersaults and hurtling upstairs.

    Chasing his tail, jumping for flies,
    lurking in flower beds, watching the skies.

    Dashing like a cheetah all through the house
    then settling on my lap, to dream of a mouse.

I'm glad he came.

David Wright

WHAT NEXT?

You know why we live in North Lancashire,
And the wonderful views we have around here.
From previous poems published by Forward Press.
What to write about now? Yes, I know - the *Mess*!

We live in a bungalow, small and complete,
It should be quite easy to keep everything neat.
Husband turns wood for a living you know
And sawdust gets everywhere - it is always on show!

Is it worth cleaning, I say to myself?
I don't dust on top of every tall shelf,
But the minute I've vacuumed and dusted around
Husband walks in and re-covers the ground.

This housewife's work is never done
As soon as she's finished she need not have begun.
There is no answer to problems like this
Twenty-four hours of clean house would be bliss!

M C Cobb

HONOURS - PRE SOCCER

In days of old, when knights were bold
and football wasn't invented.
The favourite sport was jousting.
they earned their honours ousting.

To get their rivals on the spot
they had to use their *lance-a lot*
Once this achieved, with skill and grace
a greater hazard had to face.

For back at home, and full of ire
awaits a dragon, breathing fire.
For like their counterparts today,
the wives of yore would have their say.

Instead of tasty snacks in sight
for tired steed and weary knight.
Across the moat, a voice would float,
'Your ousting about just gets my goat.'

Florence Pilkington

ALL MINE

That dog in my memory is dim, may fail,
No, not the wag of one little tail,
Taught how to walk with heavy milk can.
Forgotten the dairy, forgotten the man.
Can never forget, the jingly manner,
Those coins of old, the bob, and the tanner,
In hand, friendly, always mine,
Sovereigns of gold, just for Dad, not me.
My pounds were paper, made out of a tree,
Three pennies, a joey, such silver shine,
In puddings, for kids at Xmas time,
A florin, a two bob piece, nice old name,
A bright silver half dollar, two and six the same,
Edge, rough with milling, blind folk feel around,
Shillings of silver, just twenty in pound,
One to nineteen, and pence, price nice sound,
Six heads of royals, most older than Dad,
History in the pocket, perhaps all I had.
Libra, the gold, Solido, the silver,
Dinero, the copper, names back in time.
Our money today, has no reason or rhyme.

H Cotterill

TIME

Time can seem long, time can seem short
If you're trying to forget, it's there in thought
Sometimes a day can seem like a week
When nothing goes right . . . everything's bleak.

Time can seem good, time can seem bad
It's good when you're happy . . . but not when you're sad
When you're happy - the time seems to fly . . .
But when you're sad, watching the minutes tick by.

Time can seem wrong, time can seem right
We all live to a clock . . . wake up to daylight
It's all a vicious circle - don't be late!
Every minute, every hour, every day . . . every date.

Heather R E Cox

MY DREAMS' DESIRE

To secret bower in greeny dell
In Mytton's fair domain
Where river meet and Ribble flows
I must go there again

For now in sylvan majesty
With gnomes and faery elves
Where stately oaks stand sentinel
My dreams' desire dwells

Often in the flush of dawn
As songsters shrilly sing
With timeless grace and fleetingly
She sets them all a'wing

Up and on o'er Hodder's banks
Round through Vale of Loud
To coax the early morning sun
That pierces Pendle's cloud

Now as clammy spring morn mists
From a waking earth are shorn
God's shimmering pearl transforms the sky
To eastward and the day is born.

N A Corker

VISIONS

Your face lights up at the start of the day
Smiling widely like a sunlight ray
You move gracefully in the breezy air
Dancing without music or without care
I look at you and my heart sings out
With tenderness and love there is no doubt
I feel so happy just looking at you
As many others must feel the same too
You are so beautiful lying in your bed
Surrounded by colour, purple, blue and red
I must leave you but long to hold you near
To smell your perfume every day of the year
You are not alone when you sleep at night
Shielding your face awaiting the daylight
How sad a place the world would surely be
Without the beauty of a flower outside to see.

Barbara D Price

ARTHRITIS

The pain is bad in whichever place,
not only in the human race.
Can cripple and hurt many a life,
not only the husband, but also the wife.
Painkillers, keep warm they say, there's no cure,
but this will help, and I'm not sure.
When the weather's bad it really moves in,
if I could wrap it up, it would go in the bin.
It can run in the family, this I fear,
I know the pain and persevere.
Inflammation of a joint called arthritis,
it's one thing in life I wouldn't miss.

L Atherton

NIGHTMARE

The door creaked open to his knock
And there she stood, dear God, the shock.
Unfocussed eyes of summer blue
Her punctured skin a deathly hue.

She turned the key within the lock
And stepping naked from the frock
That fell with dreadful practised ease,
She said, 'Do with me as you please.'

Her slender arms coiled round his neck
Her tarnished head beneath his chin,
He stroked her bare and lovely back
And cursed the horror 'neath her skin.

He'd held this body one day old,
Had bathed and kissed each chubby fold,
Had tucked her in and stories told
And shared a love more pure than gold.

Those fleeting years beyond compare
That baby, child, then woman fair,
Into the eager world she flew
Quenched burning wings with devil's brew.

'When once we fed the hens, my dear,'
He whispered to unheeding ear,
'Then you would hide your face and cry
When I said some sick chick must die.'

'My little bird, I love you so
My life I'll give to let you go.'
His strong hands raised her golden head
A twist, a click, and she was dead.

Casey Aitch

WITCH'S BREW

She sits in a corner
In a tall black hat
'Reading' spells, on this and that
Her green eyed cat,
Asleep on a mat, near
A crackling log fire,
That sounds like frogs,
Near a door, her broomstick
Awaiting midnight.
At the bewitching hour,
And swish of her cape
She's away, up high, on her broomstick
Up in the sky.
Twice round the moon
Past the north star
Just missing Jupiter and Mars.
Then back over the tree tops
With such a scowl
Just missing tawny owl.
Back to her hovel before daylight
To conjure up more spells
For Hallowe'en night.

Margaret Parnell

TIME

Time is a word we all fear
Time is a word that brings a tear
As we all remember times gone b y
and we all ask questions, where? Why?

I am a sixteen year old girl looking through a mirror and what do I see
I see an old lady looking back at me
Where did that young girl disappear to, she went in the blink of an eye
That is how fast time passes by

Time is going faster, the years are too few
Don't look at me like that, it's happening to you too
I've written a list of what I want to do
You must do the same, all of you!

J Roberts

SEA MOODS

Oh beautiful and turbulent sea
How I often think of thee,
Sometimes calm, sometimes rough,
Laughing, leaping on the shore.

Today is calm and so serene,
Tomorrow may be a different scene.
Sea horses of white foam leap,
As the wind hastens their retreat.

Lovely colours come to mind,
Azure blue, navy, turquoise, grey,
As waves dance along the bay,
It's like a dream on display.

Castle walls have kept thee out,
From the turret one can peep,
As battleships approach the keep,
Might sea you may not enter.

Artists, many a canvas painted,
Fantasy as well as true,
So I will relinquish thee,
To many moods of the sea.

Kathleen Gosling

What Is Yellow?

Yellow is the sun
Bold and bright
Yellow is a candle
Shining in the night.

Yellow is the sound
Of an Easter chick cheeping
Yellow is the newborn
Lambs, jumping and leaping.

Yellow is a daffodil
Growing in the sun
Yellow is a sunflower
Sowed one by one.

Yellow is calm, soft
And warm
Yellow is tranquillity
Fresh from the dawn.

Lorraine Dick (13)

Calder Vale

I went for a walk and met a cat strolling along the grassy path
She walked on by unhurriedly then disappeared quite suddenly.
The sun shone down on dappled ground and two small rabbits
                                 settled down to sit in the sun.
They seemed quite unaware of me, so I walked on by and let them be.
Honeysuckle filled the hedges, hanging down in golden tresses.
Butterflies and honey bees all about on this soft June day.
Not a cloud to mar the sky, peace and harmony prevail
                                 in lovely secret Calder Vale.

Lily Jeffries

NOT MANY VISITORS TODAY

A seaside town in winter.
Terraces of silent hotels,
their empty windows staring
blankly out across a gale-lashed
promenade.
Shuttered shops, all patiently waiting
for warmer days and new paint.
A hibernating place, with here and
there a statement of entrepreneurial
optimism. Reduced terms, early and late.
Centrally heated rooms: Vacancies.
The strings of multicoloured lights
flicker and dance about, high in the
windy streets. And the harbour empty,
but for a few small fishing boats
waiting for the weather.
High tide, low tide. Rise and fall.
And heaven help the sailors on
a night like this.

D Taylor

SCHOOL RULES

Do you know our school rules?
They're certainly not for silly fools.
We have to wear our uniform with pride,
Not allowed to have bikinis outside,
And have to be at school on time,
But I can't find another word to rhyme.
And don't forget not to hit, bully or fight,
Or you will be sure to get a fright.

Kirsty Leighton (9)

MISTER SNOOZE

On the roller coaster
   He hears 'Aahs!' and 'Oohs!'
White-knuckled, the people -
   But *not* Mister Snooze.

While kids scream by mothers
   When the going's steep,
Wedged between two others,
   Our hero's asleep . . .

Inside the Haunted House -
   Chain-clanking - and groans -
Each sudden ghoul or ghost
   Meet only his yawns.

Returning by the train,
   He closes one eye,
Once again, nodding off,
   His stop flashes by . . .

Others may climb mountains,
   Exclaim at the view,
Back on his balcony,
   Guess what he will do . . .

He's booked his next holiday
   He'll go on a cruise -
The perfect way for him
   To have one long snooze.

When his name is called out
   On the last Judgement Day,
Some Archangel will find
   Him snoring away.

C Creedon

WOLF'S MESSAGE TO MAN

A sound from the wilderness could once be heard
A most awesome sound of a beast
Who lived free, as free as a bird

Then man came along, as he watched and observed
He felt a strong need
A purpose he had to fulfil
To tame the wild beast
Who hunted with skill

So narrowed was the gulf 'tween man and wolf
As you ate your free meal
Then by the warmth of the fire
In your innocence lay
Having no idea of the price
Your offspring would have to pay

When man came along
Can anyone explain what went wrong
Dog found man could be
So unjust in his dealing, in man's imperfection
He failed to see the need
To understand canine communication

There is a call from the wild
Echoing down from the past
A most haunting sound
'Tis wolf's message to man!
Listen to my offspring if you possibly can!

Listen with your eyes! Watch! Do observe,
My offspring the dog needs to be heard
He has a need to be understood
So please close the gulf
'tween man and wolf.

Hilary Turner

The Silence Of Winter

A shaft of sunlight struggles through the curtain
Outside the birds face the icy blasts
The silent snowy world seems to whisper
Wondering perhaps whether anyone will venture
Into the unknown and survive the elements

Two figures emerge from the mist
One is small but forceful in their steps
The other is bent and sheltering from the wind
A man and his dog appear
The snow falls once again
Leaving no trace of their footsteps
The silent world returns

Betsey Prose

The Weed

I'm on about the dreaded curse,
The ciggy, so to speak,
I talked my dearest better half,
To toss the filthy weed.

He did - to my amazement,
And I really should feel glad,
But all I feel is guilty,
And also pretty bad.

You see - I haven't cracked it yet,
I haven't really tried,
Each ciggy that I smoke is last,
Each time, I know I've lied.

But what I'm really saying,
And not too well I fear,
Tomorrow is another day,
Let's hope success is near.

M Goodier

DISTANT ADMIRER

The moon -
His eyes, forever gazing in awe at Mother Earth
Would be, if life became extinct, the only witness.
He waltzes around her, as she pirouettes her way
Through the immense ebony ballroom of space.
Throughout the night, a vigil he keeps,
While upon the Earth, her inhabitants sleep.
Being a true gentleman, if I may say,
He makes himself scarce during the day.
From Earth's clinging arms, he can never be free,
So strong her attraction to him it be.
Companion, and hostage, and Earth's chaperone,
He makes his power felt, and his presence known.
By affecting our moods,
And turning the tides,
Are just two of the ways
He controls our lives.
But, sometimes with Earth, he wants to play tricks,
He treats her inhabitants to a solar eclipse.
Her witness to life,
Her partner in dance,
By the moon -
Mother Earth, was highly romanced.

Martin Howard

ON BEING A PARENT

'The Ecstasy and the Agony'
Is the best way to describe
The feeling of a parent
When bringing up a child

That precious, purest moment
As new life comes to this world
But be careful of the chaos
As into sleepless nights you're hurled

There's no more doubt about it
They will really drive you wild
As one moment they're like Jekyll
And the next they're just like Hyde

There's nothing quite so wondrous
As that huge broad beaming smile
But savour that rare moment
It only happens once a while

They are totally demanding
When a babe or in their teens
They expect you to do everything
But *please* don't iron their jeans!

They go through lots of stages
In those twenty years or so
You think you've finally worked them out
You haven't really though

You scream and shout, you nag and moan
There's nothing they do right
It seems you have an alien being
Who stays out late each night

Yet in the final analysis
There's nothing shines above
From a parent and its offspring
Comes that pure, eternal love

Leila Caryll

ESCALATORS

I often wonder why we don't change,
And give up cars of every range.
To enhance the atmosphere
We could have roads full of trees,
Lovely plants and clean air please.
How would we travel to and fro,
On escalators built in pavements on which
               young and old could go.
Stepping on and off again,
No quick or slow lane. Just a speed for one and all,
To get on and off without a fall.
Trains could still be used,
To carry people far without abuse.
A healthier nation we would be,
Living life more naturally.
I know it seems impossible now,
But who knows exactly how
This world of ours, will take the final bow,
Saving animals like the cow.
No more dreaded disease,
They will have a life of ease.
So let us remember the escalator,
Could make the world as intended,
               by its Creator.

M E Ashley

SNOBBY

A pedigree poodle was prancing about
When out of the park he heard a loud shout
'Hello little darling, fancy a smooch'
'Not on your life, you scruffy old pooch'
'Oh come over here, I'll tickle your belly'
'Shove off you mongrel, you're scruffy and smelly'
'See you my luv you're too high and mighty'
'Better than you, you're fruity and flighty'
'Oh come over here, let's do what dogs do'
'I'd rather be dead than do things with you'
'Come on luv, let's go for a walk'
'Go for a walk? You can't even talk'
'See me and you, we'd make a great twosome'
'Oh my dear god! The thought is just gruesome'
'Come home with me, meet the rest of the clan'
'I wouldn't go nowhere with you my young man'
'If you come over here, I'll give yer a biscuit'
'Not on your life, I wouldn't dare risk it'
The mongrel's advances were beginning to wane
When out of the wood came a dirty Great Dane
He pounced on the poodle, on to her back
A wicked, ferocious awful attack.
The poodle, she shouted, she shouted for aid
The mongrel responded, although real afraid
It was bloody and brutal, a terrible fight
Kicking and scratching and bite after bite
The mongrel had won, the Great Dane took off
Now to the poodle the mongrel's a toff
The poodle she said 'How would you like a hug'
The mongrel replied 'I'd rather nibble your lug.'

B Boertien

MILLENNIUM NIGHT

Millennium, millennium
Hip, hip, hooray
Special year, special day
Past, present, future bright
Which cometh around
This millennium night

Water's edge, along our prom
Albert dock for everyone
Music sounds from far, wide
Bards marching at our side
Marquees fairground
Stalls an' all
Come and have a ball

Fireworks light up the sky
People passing by
Dancing, singing merrily so
Different balloons up, up, they go
Silver, white, millennium night

Magic in the air
Two thousand years
Jesus was here
He gave life to all behold
That's a story been told
Light a candle, say a prayer
Remembering we can share

Stroke of midnight
Oh those bells
Ring out cheers
Wishes wells

Gail Rowan

AN INDUSTRIAL REVOLUTION

Our industries are crying out
in blood and sweat and tears
Despite the skills and expertise
passed down throughout the years
Our heritage was formed by those
who strove so we could gain
That we would carry on their skills
and carry on their name

Proud men and women their backs bent low
resigned unto their task
Produced the finest merchandise
that anyone could ask
From early morn to late at night
together side by side
Some twelve and fourteen hours they toiled
in order to survive

Now our industries are dying
crying out in shame
They're slipping through our fingers
like water down a drain
And with it goes our heritage
our right to carry on
A decent way to earn our pay
as our ancestors have done

Redundancies and closures
recession and a slump
These words we've heard so many times
how many more to come
As doors close all around us
how many more will fall?
How many more will join the queues
already on the dole?

Pauline Tattersall

CUCKOO LAND

Kick your feet through daffodil dust
take up a porcupine's time
you may believe the world is flat
own a cat that's older than nine

Measure the size of six thousand flies
with a tape four inches long
a chameleon with no camouflage
finds it hard to hide his tongue

Rhyme a word like orange
they say it can't be done
oh yes it can, oh yes it can
try sporange says my mum

Here, there and everywhere
and underneath the sea
upside down and inside out
have a cuttlefish stay for tea.

Read a paper that's been red
or was it green or was it blue
but news to you is news to me
so no news must be true

Jump up and down, jump up and down
and then jump side to side
shear a sheep then dye the wool
knit a pavement three feet wide

Go on, go on I hear you say
go on strike up the band
I'd rather be here than anywhere
turn left for Cuckoo Land.

Jake

THE FLOWER FESTIVAL

For weeks and weeks we spent many hours,
Learning how to arrange the flowers.
Each Tuesday night we met in the hall,
Oasis and flowers, leaves, containers and all.

We would fix, take out and arrange again,
And nothing appeared to sink into our brain.
Then all at once it seemed to click,
Our leaders teaching had done the trick.

Then as the great day drew nearer and nearer,
Our classes increased to make things clearer,
And we all declared we would do our best,
Thursday June 2nd would be the test.

Outside the church there were buckets of flowers,
And all kinds of foliage, we worked for hours,
We did window arrangements, pew ends were done,
Topiary trees, screens decorated, we all worked as one.

There were bookmarks for the choir stalls, using pressed flowers,
The church was transformed in a matter of hours.
The fellowship was wonderful, how it uplifts,
As we worked to the glory of God with our gifts.

We worked very hard, from morning till night,
But everything had to be just right.
At last it was finished, we had done our best,
Thankfully we went home to rest.

E Kay

AFTER THE SIEGE

Night full of noise and incessant conflict
sleep a distant memory
Liars camp outside my home
smashing my windows with every twisted fact
Friends shake their heads and blame my attitude
or speculate 'It could be a lesson from God'
My wife builds strongholds of hatred around her heart
and prays for the day when I am gone
Enemies re-load their weapons
and laugh at the tears of this broken man

At every turn a closed door
On every song a scar
Every moment owns a sigh
but no one calls
no one comes
no visitors allowed in this war zone

I crawl across the debris of what was my life
and it turns to dust in my hands
I shout to distant strangers on another shore
but they turn and walk away

I try to find some water in this barren land
but the tornado of unforgiveness has dried up every stream
Despair lights the fuse and walks away

Alone

Silence descends
A lifetime of relationships and passers by
watch my body to see
When I lift my eyes to them
'Who will I be?'

Stephen Starkie

LIFE IN A CARING COMMUNITY

Life in a caring community
Is a happy place to be
People who lend a helping hand
And the time to enjoy life is free.
The farmers plough the fields
And the sun is shining in the sky
The cultural heritage that is here before me
There's lots of reasons why.
The church clock that strikes
And the time is finally here
Praying to each and every one of us
That we do from year to year.
The young people who live in the village
Are as friendly as can be
Living life up to the full
It's absolutely free.
The greengrocer that serves the old lady
And the baker who serves the young man
The caring people that come to help
They'll be with us while they can.
The people who are retired
And the time is finally here
People who have worked all their lives
And to enjoy another year.
The garden is a picture of success
I think that you might say
Dreaming of the glorious days of summer
And living it up all through the day.

C Kirkham

LOCAL PAPERS

How I love the local news,
The price of beef, the editors' views,
Who's in trouble with the law,
Haven't I read that name before?

Who has died, what age were they?
Which house is sold, what did they pay?
All this - and more, we read each week,
(The gossip page - with tongue in cheek!)

On holiday, to the newsagents go I,
The local papers, there to buy,
To get a feeling of the place,
The vagrancies of the human race!

Returning home, what's my first task?
Why! To read the news, need you ask?
Astonished to find, it didn't say,
That yours truly had been away!

The small ads grab my attention,
Is it true, or an invention?
Do they really have such things for sale?
Unwanted gifts! Oh! what a tale!

He's made them all, one at a time,
Can't fool a nosy mind like mine!
A garage sale from year to year,
Daily there, new goods appear!

Now I read an obituary,
Have they prepared one for me?
I think I'll ask that the local paper,
Is in my box, when I meet my maker!

Brian Humphreys

WILD HORSES

Onward, forever onward,
They thunder through the night;
They leap and kick, and twist and turn,
Until they're out of sight.
Their ghostly shapes, they seem so big,
As they cross the 'great divide';
Through the dust they make, I can hardly see,
Though my eyes are open wide.
They stop to drink, then thunder on,
To where, remains untold?
For their restless spirit can't be tamed,
Even in the nightly cold.
Their distant shapes have gone from sight,
But the noise still lingers on;
As it rides the wind from where it came,
And rests, now that they're gone.

B Colebourn

RIVINGTON PIKE

If you want to go for a hike
Get your boots and walk to Rivington Pike
It could take you just over an hour
On a clear day you can see Blackpool Tower

The walk is hard, the going is tough
No proper paths and in parts it's rough
If you wear boots you will be all right
When you reach the top a fantastic sight

Cars on the motorway look like toys
You're too far away to hear any noise
Rest for a while and take in the terrain
Take in some air before walking down again

If you want to go for a hike
Get your boots and walk to Rivington Pike
It could take you just over an hour
On a clear day you can see Blackpool Tower

J Morris

CASTLEMAINE

Oh, I remember Castlemaine
And riding the old rickety train
With wooden slatted seats and doors
And in the carriage smoke would pour.
Rattling slowly up the range
Every turn a landscape change
Till at last we reach the top
And then we walk until we drop.
    Barefoot in the mountain stream
    A pleasure you can only dream
    And drink the sweet wine from the hill
    Like dew from heaven to take your fill
And then to lie in purple hue
Entwined till darkness falls
Like a mantle to conceal
Until the morning dawn.
    Then sleep the sleep that only lover's know
    Until the stark and light of day
    Time to reap what we have sown
    But the wonder would remain.
How deep the love that we had found
As we trod the heathery ground
Two different people we become
As we rode the rickety train
Down the hills from Castlemaine.

Jean Carter

FOND MEMORIES OF OLD FRIENDS

It is sometimes mindful, to remember things of old,
When families really struggled to keep out the cold.

A bag of coal, costing as much as two bob,
And people fought on doing a hard grafting job.

To toil and struggle then, was a tough task indeed,
But toil they did, to fulfil their children's needs.

I think back to nineteen thirty-nine, starting work in the pit,
At fourteen years of age, feeling so proud and so fit.

With peaked cap, water can and Tommy tin as well,
And stepping into the pit cage, to descend into hell.

This was Blundell's Colliery, one of Wigan's mines of old,
Where the miners slogged, digging for that precious black gold.

And those great pit pal lads, that I clearly recall,
Like Joe Sweeney, Tommy Fairhurst, Bobby Irvine and all.

Tom Bilsborough, Jim Sharrock, Bill Ratchford, come to mind,
All great work buddies, as good as you could find.

Richard Hurley, was another of the old pit gang,
And all of them willing to give a helping hand.

There was also Tommy Kelly, a true and loyal mate,
All of us argued sometimes without feeling any hate.

Progress through our early teens, was the pony driving stage,
It also helped to bring home, a slightly better wage.

Sixteen years old then, and still eager to learn more,
Driving those hard working ponies, was never a bore.

Keen for the shift to be over, and back to the Pit-E,
Then soar up to the surface, that wonderful sky to see.

Some of these great guys, have now sadly passed away,
But stay forever in our thoughts, with each passing day.

So to all the younger relatives, of the lads named above,
You can look up to them with pride, and parental love.

Ernest Melling

MY TIGER CUBS

On wint'ry days, cold, wet and dark,
When storm-tossed clouds becloak blue skies,
My soul reflects upon that spark,
Struck deep within their lustrous eyes.

Light up my heart with feline fire
And let me hear contented purr;
Recall to mind that keen desire,
To see their striped, symmetric fur!

Wide-spreading paws and white-tipped ears -
That twitch of whiskers, flick of tails -
Bring smiles to lips and banish tears;
My sunny mood again prevails.

They run and tumble, spirits fired,
Then rest awhile, 'neath shady tree.
The morning's play has made them tired,
My tiger cubs, so wild and free.

A shadow now thru' tall grass strays;
Rahjina growls from nearby shrubs.
Proud, untamed eyes towards me blaze,
As she reclaims my tiger cubs.

Gareth Wynne Richards

THE HIGHFALUTIN SCOTSMAN

I'm a highfalutin Scotsman
Keepin' up ancestral ways:
A-huntin' and a-fishin'
Is my highland game that pays:
Though my kilt is worn and faded:
And my sporran's moulted bare:
I'm a highfalutin Scotsman
Sought by gentry everywhere:
With thistle in my bonnet and a twinkle in my eye
I'm a highfalutin Scotsman, from the bonny Isle of Skye.

I'm a highfalutin Scotsman
With an ever lovin' wife:
A braw wee lass, and canny
From the ancient town of Fife:
With a pheasant, trout and salmon
There's no cook that can compare:
She's a highfalutin lady
With a larder never bare.
With thistle in my bonnet and a twinkle in my eye
I'm a highfalutin Scotsman, from the bonny Isle of Skye.

I'm a highfalutin Scotsman:
Master of the secret ways:
I share the throne of eagles
'Mid sweet heathers purple blaze:
Skylark pipes a merry welcome
As I wend my royal way:
I'm a highfalutin Scotsman
Thankin' God for every day.
With thistle in my bonnet and a twinkle in my eye
I'm a highfalutin Scotsman, from the bonny Isle of Skye.

Violet M Corlett

Remembrance

I have gone away from here,
I've travelled on before you.
Weep not for me, my precious love,
No tears of grief, no sorrow.

I'm just absent for a while,
Yet with you, hand in hand;
My fragrant presence by your side,
In everything you do.

Remember me in springtime, love,
As snowdrop's pearly head
Offers up in pale sun's gleam,
Its kiss of sacred innocence.

A full blown rose of summer,
Its heady scent a message
Blown on the wind, to tell you,
I'm waiting here for you!

Children blossomed from our love,
Flourished from our garden;
Mourn no more in autumn's shades,
No falling tears, summer's leaves.

My laughter's in a playful breeze,
Sad tears in April's rain;
Midday's sun, a warm embrace,
A melting kiss, a snowflake's form.

Hear my whisper in the trees,
My distant voice in ocean's roar;
At night, look skyward to the stars,
I'm waiting here for you, my love!

Jill Gems

EVENTIDE

The sun went down behind the hill,
The birds flew home to rest,
A sighing wind caressed the trees,
That God with leaves had blessed.
A cloudless sky with stars bedecked,
Like jewels shining bright,
The messy banks with dew were flecked,
The herald of the night,
So hushed in sleep the birds and trees,
For another day is done,
To awaken with the buzzing bees,
And the rising of the sun.
When dawn breaks o'er the eastern sky,
Once more to life they spring,
'Tis then you hear the song birds cry,
And the lark upon the wing,
There's beauty all around us,
Every minute of the day,
But how few of us take notice
Of God's countryside display.

Eric McBride

LORD, I THANK THEE!

For Loving me in a very Special way -
    Lord, I thank Thee!
For Guiding me aright, from day to day -
    Lord I thank Thee!

For the many Blessings You've showered on me,
    Lord, I thank Thee!
For cutting the chains of Bondage, to set me free -
    Lord, I thank Thee!

For the beauty I see, in all Your Creations -
    Lord, I thank Thee!
For shared happy moments, with friends and relations -
    Lord, I thank Thee!
For the little miracles I watch enfolding -
    Lord, I thank Thee!
From this day forth, until Your Precious Face I'm beholding -
    Lord I thank Thee!

M Ross

A POEM FOR PEACE

All over this world, for every colour and creed,
The most sinful things in life, are *power, hate* and *greed.*
They cause unhappiness and bloodshed, and awful loss of life,
They lead to war and conflicts, and to dreadful grief and strife.

All over this world, most people pray for *peace.*
We ask for worldwide *love,* and let the wars all cease.
Unite mankind to realise, that to *share* will be the victory,
When power, hate and greed are gone, the world will all be free.

All over this world, for all of the tomorrows,
There is hope for future happiness and easing of all sorrows.
Pray for all who suffer, in their war of bomb and gun,
That they will be comforted, and know that *love* has won.

All over this world, whether black , or yellow, or white,
May the God you put your faith in, be your guiding light.
May He be your beacon, showing you to be honest, giving and kind,
So that you will feel true happiness, with joyful, peaceful mind.

All over this world, *goodness* and *mercy* must win,
So that every colour, creed and age, will then know peace within.
This is a poem for *peace,* and a dream for all to *share,*
It is a wish for everyone, to trust, agree, and to really *care.*

Pauline Mole

ALAN JAMES

He came into this world
A baby o' so fair
But as the years went by
He was a real Dan Dare.

No lock or key could hold him
He was a little (B)
But the smile and love upon his face
Was there for all to see.

To get him to help was a problem
Work just wasn't his style
When it came to planting tatties
He just disappeared for a while.

Then he got a motor bike
And love was in the air
Up to Ambleside he did go
And wed without a care.

Soon there were two little Coopers
Who Alan took to his heart
But at weekends you would find him
Somewhere with a Quickstart.

But life wasn't all roses
And back to mam he went
She said, 'Why don't you try again?'
So up he got and went.

He built himself a brand new house
And lived there all alone
Till love tapped at the window
And made it home sweet home.

Then he became a grandad
He really wasn't old
But beneath that old rough coat
There lay a heart of gold.

Daisy Cooper

INNOCENT EYES

From the TV screen an orphaned child
Stares at me with bewildered, tear filled eyes.
I turn away to eat my tea and momentarily avert my mind.
Like a magnet, my ear's drawn to the reporter's voice
Hear the immoral horrors of genocide,
And suppressing tears, a lump wells in my throat,
As I feel for the young orphan boy,
And a life that he has now left behind.
An orphaned child stares back at me
As I lay in bed at night,
Trying to bury deep inside an image I cannot hide.
Tear stained dirt upon their face
And fear within their eyes,
Shattered souls coldly numbed by propaganda lies.
Tiny hands grip a barbed wire fence,
Their desperate eyes stare out beyond
From mud filled fields of tents.
Cold and weak from days and nights of walking
Their silent faces torn with pain,
Their shredded feet now wrapped in rags,
Does all the talking.
From the TV screen an orphaned child
Stares at me and every other nation,
Remembrance day's forgotten now,
Again - humanitarian devastation.

Greg King

OLD PALS

Stars light up a black velvet sky,
Moonbeams dance, as he sails by.
Alone in his trusty boat,
Old fisherman in his tattered coat.

A large fish, his prey,
Many times has got away.
Whilst weathered old hands are hook baiting,
A fish is watching and waiting.

Take up my challenge, show me your face,
Line jerks, fish leaps, boat increases pace.
Face to face now, knowing their fate,
Their eyes show admiration, not hate.

Tired, bleeding hands hold fast the line,
Far out to sea, joined together in time.
Battle now over, both cradled by waves,
Happy together in watery graves.

Far below, two old pals lie,
Above the sea birds cry.
Stars take flight after watching the show,
As dawn breaks, with a golden glow.

Violet Robinson

SUNSET

Across the plains I see it
The sun setting in the distance.
Orange colours calm and cool bright sky.
It is just like my mother, soft and gentle.
I wish it would stay with me and my mother as well.

Ruth Waters (9)

THE 25TH DECEMBER

Two days before the big event, there's a multitude of shoppers.
I need something gold for Uncle Joe,
Scented perfume for Auntie Mary,
And a toy lamb for cousin Luke.

Then comes the wrapping up escapade.
How in heaven or on earth do you wrap a toy lamb?
In swaddling clothes? No, a box is best.
Have I a box? I have . . . I know I have . . .

The night before the event of great joy, we go out.
It's the usual ritual,
A drink at one pub, then the next,
We move on, but there's no room at 'The Inn'.

After the meal,
We sit holding the family's first born son,
Vowing never to eat as much ever again.
The New Year's resolution (again).

Two days after Christmas, there's a new multitude,
This time of bargain hunters.
We see the signs, shining like the star,
Sale! Sale! Sale!

Queuing outside in the drizzle,
No White Christmas this year.
Must have that dress, must have these shoes . . .
Spend, spend, spend.

Is that what Christmas is really about?
What happened to that precious event all those years ago?

Kathryn Millington

IMAGINE IF TREES COULD TALK...
(For Dad)

I wish I could see
what a tree can see
I wish I could be
where a brick could be
Imagine all that history
that's gone by
A decade, a century
a lifetime that's passed
Unnoticed, unseen, gone
at the drop of a hat
But imagine, just imagine
if trees could talk
What a wonderful story
of days of old
A full account of history
never to be told.

Maria Waters

THE PATH OF LIFE

The path of life is long and rough
Sometimes hard, sometimes very tough
But life has to go on however rough
Everybody has to take the smooth with the rough,
But life doesn't get any easier, however tough.
It breaks hearts and causes families to fight,
No one knows who's wrong or right,
The path of life has no light
Only ill feelings among those who fight,
This is the path of life,
Proving there's no wrongs or rights.

S Johnson

MOTHERS

When she gives birth to a child
She sketches her dreams of wild

She prepares it with tender love and care
To see her masterpiece in world's fare

When that masterpiece grows up and steps outside
Leaves an empty space deep inside

That is the fate of mothers world wide
Give your love, heart, soul and step aside

Watch them create their own little worlds
Remember, your grief, heart break to hide

Mothers are artists and creators of tomorrow
So they watch world's reaction in surprise

Ruby Khan

MILLENNIUM HOPES

As it comes ever near,
The millennium year,
What can we hope for anew.
Not riches or wealth,
But peace and good health,
And love between friends so true.
Let bygones be bygones, between countries at war.
Let's all work for each other's well being.
Take each other's hand,
United to stand,
And give thanks to God the all-seeing.

Kathleen Catterall

DESTRUCTION

Wrap me warm in yesterday
that I may languish still.
Let time be stopped forever,
for tomorrow holds a chill.
A world of silent fury,
of fields no longer green.
A land that bears no fruit,
a desecrated scene.
Barren trees and arid oceans
lie heavy on the ground.
A sky of hopeless grey
falls down without a sound.
The air is thick and rancid,
filled with the cries of death.
And Mother Earth emits a sigh
as she takes her final breath!

L Jones

HAUSFRAU

To be treated humanely is not much to ask
She'd like to grab hold and take you to task
Deplore her, ignore her, she just wants to know
Is she still wanted
Or should she just go?
Chief cook, bottle washer, cleaner and fool
Is she no longer this home's little jewel?
See to the washing
See to the meals
Who gives a damn just how she feels?

Janette Harazny

Autumn

Sometime in the night,
Silent and unseen,
The autumn wizard
Transformed all the green.

He worked his magic,
Used his palette well,
Eye catching colours
Cast on all a spell.

Red and gold dancing,
Sunlight catches leaves,
Yellow, orange, brown,
Through them all he weaves.

Like precious metals,
Bronze and copper sheen
Glints in the sunlight,
Sets the autumn scene.

Sometime in the night,
When no one was there,
The wind blew the leaves
Making branches bare.

Gone is the magic,
The trees are all black,
Wait for next autumn,
Wizard will be back.

Angela Pritchard

The Reluctant Master

I don't want to be a sailor,
Or a fireman, brave and strong.
I don't want to be a soldier
And fight the whole day long.
I don't want to be a cowboy,
Or a silly Indian Chief!
I don't want to be a teacher,
Or a dentist filling teeth.
I don't want to be a banker,
Not manager, nor clerk.
I don't want to be a miner
And stay down in the dark!

I want to be a gentleman
And dine with gentle folk.
I want a chef and butler man
And eggs without a yolk.
I want a maid to clean my clothes
And a slave to clean my shoes.
I want someone to wipe my nose
And never blow a fuse.
I want someone to make my bed
And never push and shove.
I want someone to soothe my head
And fill my world with love.

- Oh mummy dear, my mummy dear,
I don't want to be grown up!
Mummy dear, please hear, please hear:
I'm still your little pup!

Kathryn J Hayward

ETHNIC CLEANSING

Why oh why can't people see
What these wars mean to you and me
Men who pillage, rape and plunder
Bringing misery to all and sunder
What oh what is it all for
This crazy thing that they call war
The innocent people that are dying
Why do men refrain from trying
Ethnic cleansing is the new name it's given
From their homes the people are driven
Murdered, raped and left to die
People's spirits can't reach the sky
Heartache and misery for those left behind
All due to the greed of all mankind
Turn of the news good people say
But it will be there still, the very next day

Patricia Davis

HUBBY'S RETIREMENT

You thought that your retirement years would be a complete doddle,
Well! my dearest husband put that idea right out of your noddle.
The lawn it needs a mowing, the windows need a clean,
The car it is so dirty, it has lost its lovely sheen.
The tap it needs a washer to stop its little drip,
Then there is some rubbish to take down to the tip.
The caravan it needs a wash and a polish too,
Weeds in the front garden are pushing their way through.
The path it needs a brushing and the bushes need a prune,
So, this my dearest husband is why I am singing you this tune.

Joan P Mayer

CROSS-COUNTRY

It was February the 3rd, 1998
I was walking the course with Katie - my mate
The mud was seeping through my new spikes
This is the dry part - help, oh yikes!
Well we stood in the pen, all rearing to go
When it started to rain
The reaction was 'So!'
The gun was fired and we began to run
There was nothing to warm us - not even the sun
I was running and running
For what felt like forever
I was determined to finish, despite of the weather
There were loads of people in front of me
They were just blobs of rain from what I could see
Then from out of the rain came the finish line
(It was very obvious, because of a sign)
I started to sprint as fast as I could
I'd finish it now - I knew I would
Well I did, and I was 16th place
So that was it, the end of the race.

Holly Stewart (12)

UNTITLED

I am the mightiest of all
Low on the ground you humbly fall
And meekly to my presence crawl.

You know not what your fate may be
As fearfully you gaze on me
For I am terrible to see.

All the world now understands
The fate of all is in my hands
For I am ruler of the lands.

Now, hear the judgement which I gave:
In vain for mercy may you crave
For I, alone, have power to save.

The human wreck stared straight ahead;
He understood not what he said;
His mind and soul had long been dead.

Nigel Miller

A Letter To Sandy From Badger

At the end of the path, there's a little brown house,
and it's only one flower tall.
And I know who lives there, though he's hard to see
'cause he hides when little boys call.
There's a quaint pixie roof of straw coloured thatch,
and a quaint pixie door with a silver apple latch.
You have to know the secret that opens up the door,
and that's a tiny silver key that's hidden on the floor.
It's underneath a flower pot that stands beneath a tree,
but I don't think you will find it if you don't go there with me.
When Pixie sees it's Badger and I've brought a friend to tea,
he'll say we're very welcome and we'll join the company.
The witch from Barnswood Hollow and the fairies will be there,
'cause they always call on Fridays when they've been to Goblin Fair.
We'll have honey cakes and tansy cakes and spicy bread for tea,
and thimbles filled with berry juice, a treat for you and me!
And afterwards we'll thank them all, and they'll say 'Call again,
we'd love to see you anytime you come to Fairy Glen.'
And we'll leave a tiny parcel for Pixie by his door,
a little scent of primrose, to thank him just once more.

I Moor

A Special Invitation

Oh blackbird come again to sing
Your songs of cheer and joy;
And your sweet cousins bring -
The thrush - you never shall annoy.

Your footprints I've seen in the cold, cold snow,
Like arrows pointing to a warmer place;
After blizzards, the pale sun will show,
Please come, and our gardens grace.

I've seen you hopping over summer hedges,
And heard you pinking, pink, pink, pink;
Beneath azure skies your music wedges
Contentment, allowing us time to think.

How you startled me late this morning,
With your alarming battle cry;
For your choral work at dawning
I forgive you, 'twas a feast for ear and eye.

You gave a superb recital in the gloaming,
Competing with your feathered friends;
I strode past to buy beer afoaming -
Your singing - my quenching - with heaven blends.

James Conboy

Till Death Us Do Part

It's not nice to know you have lived a lie,
Not nice to know on the day that you die!

It's too late now to cry and moan,
The life you had was only on loan.

Something to borrow, later to return,
Yours to live truly, not yours to spurn.

As each day dawned you vowed you would act,
But time and again you honoured the pact,

And failed to escape matrimonial strife,
Failed to take hold of your wasting life,

And now - as your past before you flashes,
It's a lie that you see, and then you are ashes.

Thomas Evason

HARVEY

Once upon a time lived Harvey the bunny
Exploring the fields, he looked so funny
His little white bobtail high in the air
Warning his pals of an impending snare.

Predators lurking, all waiting to pounce
Dodging them all with his hop, skip and bounce
A fox in the bush, an eagle sky high
A cat on the prowl, lurking very close by.

A very brave buck, protecting his doe
On guard at their warren with babies in tow
A shot rings out from that enemy gun
It's the same old scenario, of run rabbit run!

He scampers through the grass, with field dogs behind
Keeping up speed, is paramount in his mind
Diving through dandelions, as quickly as he can
Will anyone save him from this gun wielding man?

A burrow looms large where his friends lie in wait
They come to his rescue, what a kind twist of fate
Harvey survived to live another day
Until he left his meadow, the natural way!

Jill Gorman

DEAR MOLLY

We've been on our holidays, grandpa and me,
We stayed in a house quite near to the sea.
The weather was sunny,
We didn't need socks
As we played in the sand
And clambered up rocks.
Each day we found treasure,
A shell or a view,
A horse in a field
And a cow that went 'moo'.
A garden with flowers
That made my eyes 'pop',
A friendly wee robin
That went 'hippity-hop'.
On the beach little children
Built castles in sand,
Frocks tucked in their knickers
Spade and bucket in hand -
They chased the sea back -
As it claimed the dry land.
I was 'king of the castle' just for a day
And walked on the walls
As my lands I surveyed.
Sheep and lambs frolicked
In a field quite nearby,
And the trees, I'm quite sure -
Reach right up to the sky -
Where seagulls were flying
And 'calling' all day,
In that holiday week, in Llandudno, in May.

Lots of love, Grandma.

Margaret Popplewell-Vessey

TWICE THE FUN

For four years I have watched Lauren learn and grow,
A pride and joy only grandads know.
Now grandad has got another princess, 'Jasmine',
A beautiful sight to behold to touch grandad's heart
When he is getting old.
Days in the park on warm summer days,
Passing many happy hours away!
The shy little look on Lauren's face as Jasmine is kept warm,
Cleaned, and fed then tucked up ready for bed!
Teddies, dolls all now shared a lovely sister for our little girl,
Grandad's time is now well spent with his two little angels
From heaven sent.
Over their heads while they sleep the magic mobile turns
Slowly around, a fairy tale picture show that,
Like grandad's stories, you never want to end!

Ken Pendlebury

THE CURSE

I once felt unhappy and very sad
But now I'm happy and very glad
That times have changed - for better not worse
I seemed to have lost my ex-wife's curse
She cast her spell - it was very bad
It made me miserable and very sad
But now it seems like a lifetime ago
And I can say that I'm proud to know
A young lady, who loves and cares
But more than that she solemnly swears
Never to hurt or to cause me pain
But more than that - make me happy again.

Chris Longwith

A Poem For My Husband

I feel middle aged
And terribly fat
My man denies it
'I wouldn't say that.'

My hair I now colour
To hide all the grey
'Leave it natural!' he says
'I like it that way.'

My legs - short and chubby
And varicose veined
He tells me are sexy
'I've never complained.'

I've now acquired tyres -
Spare ones - two!
'What tyres?' he asks
'Oh no, no - it's not true.'

He's tall - slim and handsome
Quite a good mind
But I really do think
That man must be blind!

Chérianne Wren

Posterity

Perhaps, if we are lucky,
our children will remember us,
and then, if we have fortune's favour,
our grandchildren will, amongst the haze,
speak kindly of us,
with memories faint and distant.

But then are we consigned to oblivion,
no flowers on our graves,
no casual retelling of entertaining anecdotes,
no reminiscence on a summer's eve,
only perhaps a watch passed down,
gathering dust in some sideboard drawer.

R Colville

RAINBOW OF LIGHT

We walked to school
Broke some of the rules
Laughing and singing
Church bells ringing
Always you were there
My friend who dared and cared
Dream upon dreams, that you and I shared
Both lives running together, only we ever heard
Teenage years, through stained golden tears
Slide down through sun-streaked breakaway years
A beacon so bright in the still black of night
Kindness, love light upon light
Wedding bells chime
I was yours, you were mine
Hand in hand we danced down the passage of time
Older a little wiser, you are still by my side
Friend, soulmate towards whom I always glide
Now grey of temple, a face showing signs
Of life's hard black battle lines
Your spirit not dimmed, no not for a minute
My world would be empty, without having you in it
Our bond of friendship, never broken or sneered
Thank you my one true very special friend.

Katherine Kennedy Quaye

NORTH WEST

I belong to the north west
I delight in all the soaps
Coronation Street is terrific
And used to have all the jokes
Brookside is entertaining
Which highlights the Scouse accent
But it always ends up with the star
Being a little bent
Dame Edna is a riot
You cannot beat her wit
It doesn't matter how you feel
You have to laugh a bit
We can't brag about our surrounding
Only what's in our hearts
The nicest feelings in the world
Right from the very start

M Tickle

PRIMROSE GILL

Down Primrose Gill on a warm spring day
Dreaming dreams I wend my way
The sparkle of springtime so fair and bright
Primroses and violets a wonderful sight.

Blue skies above me, the rippling stream
Beneath my feet a carpet of green,
Birds in the treetops singing their song
Small furry rabbits hopping along.

This tranquil scene, a feeling of peace
From life's care and stresses it brings a release,
Small fairy bells in patches of blue
The joy of springtime, life starts anew.

The rippling stream wending her way
Down to the sea sparkling and gay,
Banks filled with violets and primroses fair
Down Primrose Gill this warm spring day.

Doreen Moscrop

SWAN

As it waddles towards the water
We begin to think,
Oh no
Not another ugly duckling.

When it enters the water
We begin to see,
The elegance,
The beauty.

With its neck curled up high
It glides down the river,
Leaving riplets along the water
With prowess like her Majesty.

Then it straightens its neck,
Flaps its wings
Leaving the water,
Delicately.

Now it lands with a splash,
With its neck curved majestically,
This is a swan,
The king of birds.

Orry Drinkwater (16)

MIXED FEELINGS

Again you're there, lying at ease on the couch,
How could you know the best place in the house?
That's my favourite spot when I need to relax,
But time after time my patience you tax.
Having free access to what is my own
Was one of the joys of living alone.
Now . . . because of you I'm in despair,
Knowing that I have to share.

'But why should I keep you?' answer me that,
You are a most ungrateful cat.
The day I caressed you and scratched your head
You were supposed to respond, but you bit me instead.
I, who supply you with all that you need,
I've named you Smokey, should I change it to Fiend?
'Do I bless the day you first sat at my hearth,
Or curse you because you laid siege to my heart?'

You're a loner, selfish, desire your own way,
So . . . what's the attraction, it's hard to say.
The strange fascination of those amber eyes,
Or the haunting sound of your plaintive cries.
Did your displaced plight disturb my mind,
Or could it be we're two of a kind?
Am I used to you around the house, ah!
I remember now, you got rid of the mouse.

You absented yourself for two nights and a day,
I worried, I wondered if you'd gone away.
Did I say worried? I should have been glad,
What was it with me, I must have been mad.
But . . . you keep yourself spotless I'll give you that,
And you really are a beautiful cat.
But just look at you lying there, you don't give a toss,
You came as a stray, now you're the boss.

Florence Taylor

MY DEAR OLD DAD

I think about the years flown by
When youth was given wings to fly
Not as you are but as you were
Handsome and strong with never a care
Eyes that would twinkle
With love's perfect glow
Where is that twinkle? Where did it go?
For now you just sit in a pitiful heap
Snoozing in dreamland counting your sheep
No recognition when I visit you
Just a hint of a smile or a mumble or two
Hello dad! I say in a nice loving way
But all you reply is two words - go away
The eyes of a stranger they stare into mine
Accusing it seems time after time
You mumble a torrent I do not understand
Each time that I try to hold your dear hand
Where is my father who I love so dear?
Wrapped up in this stranger who fills me with fear
What is life worth I think even more?
As I take my leave through the nursing home door
It is then that I think of the years flown on by
When all youth it was given golden wings just to fly.

Eleanor Dunn

CRIPPLE

Pity me, for my crutch
is but an excuse,
and even this is lame.

Kevin Rogers

The Village 'Bygone Days'

As I sit and reminisce of times long gone over the decades
Remembering way back and the changes which have been made
In the little village of Great Barrow where I was born
Which nestles in a tiny corner of Cheshire so neatly formed
With the River Gowy which ebbs quietly through the county's plains
And along the river banks there are still a few Roman remains.

St Bartholomew's Church on Barrow Hill has stood for centuries so
    long
Built on sandstone with foundations so sturdy and strong
Which can be seen for miles around and has never changed
Still a panoramic sight over the rural range
Looking across yonder plains towards Peckforton and Beeston castles
    on the skyline
A most wonderful view and a favourite of mine
A natural highway which will never change from the 'bygone days'.

Over the years the village has expanded with a few landmarks
    disbanded
And was so quiet in those days long gone
When the farmer with his horse ploughed those furrows - a job
    well done
Now the farms have disappeared, replaced by modern housing in
    our sphere
And the tiny cottages modernised with extensions making them twice
    their size
Also the flow of traffic through the narrow lanes approach
Has of course increased since the old stage coach
And with the closure of our little railway station
Road transport is now our only automation
So instead of the country farmyard ozone of manure
It is now carbon monoxide, which is not quite so pure.

Change can be for the better or even worse
And time will take its course
But when it is the name of a house or highway road site
It can be most confusing for the old Barrowite.
So our village with changing scenes once so quiet and remote
Now has a new generation to vote
Which I hope in the 21st century they will preserve Cheshire's welfare
And perhaps in their 'bygone days' they too will be able to compare.

Nancy Owen

A Summer Afternoon

Lying in the garden, looking at the sky,
pictures started forming as the clouds went scudding by.
A rabbit with a fluffy tail was followed by a hog,
curly-tailed and chubby, behind him came a dog.
A greyhound, thin, with spindly legs, opens its mouth to bark,
the wind increased and the animals turned into Noah's Ark.
A hearty gust transformed this boat to a three-tiered wedding cake,
which blew into a sailing ship on a choppy turquoise lake.
Jagged rocks saw off the craft, which morphed into a tree,
a willow, drooping low in a blue and white tapestry.
The sun went in, the sky turned black, the pictures clouded over,
the now dark, threatening crags had just been the White Cliffs
                                                  of Dover.
I jumped up as the raindrops fell and ran dripping through the door,
no more sunbathing for me till the sky turns blue once more!

Judi Grayson

METAMORPHOSIS

Four happy children and a log.
It's been a boat, a train and a bridge
   to cross to a magic domain.
A place to sit and rest until
   time to run and play again.

It lies there still and prone,
Where once it stood proud and tall,
With branches spreading far and wide.
In springtime perfumed with blossoms sweet.
In summer screened by myriads of leaves.
A home for birds and squirrels and countless unseen creatures.
Finding shelter in secret places among the mass of tangled twigs.

It felt the warm sun, it drank the rain,
With roots anchored deep in the dark underground
It dreamed on, surely forever safe and sound.

Until one fateful day, man came and took the dream away.
With one fell swoop the tree toppled down
Severed painfully from its roots, stripped bare of its branches.
Suddenly changed from tree to log.
Left lying there, all vibrant life gone.

But then came the children so all was not lost
And in giving joy to girl and boy,
No need to regret the past.

Elsie Gmerek

WONDERING WHAT MIGHT HAVE BEEN

A crowd's the only thing that we ever shared,
   Light-hearted banter comprised our exchanges,
And I never revealed how deeply I cared;
   We were barely closer than virtual strangers.
When our eyes met, I turned mine quickly away,
   Concealing the love they would surely have shown.
Courage I hoped for eludes me to this day;
   And now in every crowd I'm always alone.
Your warmth hasn't left me in all this long while:
   Clear memories recall all that you did and said,
Dreams find me wrapped in your arms, lost in your smile;
    Are you as perfect as you are in my head?
      How can I cope with the fact that we're apart?
      Will I ever be free? Please, give back my heart.

Kim Latham

THERE IS SADNESS IN MY MIND LORD

There is sadness in my mind Lord
Yet joy within my heart.
I feel your presence near me -
You make my dark clouds part.

There is so much I want to do
I want to share with all -
The strength which you have given me
The love which makes me tall.

No one really understands
Some may think they do
But you and I know where I am
I have put my trust in you.

Catherine Thorburn

AT BEESTON CASTLE

The sun hurts my eyes
its warmth gently lifts the daisies
I can feel the sheen on my forehead
and I shelter in your cool, proud domain
a testament to another world
so long ago, something inspiring.

Possessive of your position
commandeering the Cheshire plain
the cars driving down the lane
look like toys moved by an unseen hand
in time they will decay
and you will witness more technology.

Your sandstone towers and walls
will remember my face, and countless others
they capture your image
with cameras and camcorders
a brief moment in your lifetime;
you make me feel humble.

There is a raven calling somewhere
do you share secrets with it
whispering to the trees your stories?
I remain calm and serene in your presence
I have no need to lay siege to you.
You will be here when I am long gone.

Nikky Braithwaite

ME DAD

Me dad used to say
When he was a kid
Men were tough
And feelings well hid
To cry was a weakness
When not alone
And respect for your elders
Was a must in the home
We never had much
Was a phrase he would use
Just second-hand clothes
And another's shoes
A fire was a godsend
On a cold winter's night
A dripping butty
And a candle for light
You don't know your born
He would often say
Spoilt rotten
Not like in my day
No fancy cars
Or money to waste
You kids of today
Have it all on a plate
As I've grown older
And wiser I hope
I begin to realise
Me dad was no dope

J Brooks

CHOICES OF HEART

I breathe on the carcass bed,
You adjust you hair.
There's only one reflection,
As if I'm not there.

Then you're bathing softly,
Through the paper wall.
While morning television
Mind destroys us all.

Above us, in the windows,
All the grey men shave.
Their wives are amber puppets
Waiting to enslave.
It's coronary one,
Coronary two.
It's coronary both ways
For me and for you.

I hate that evil raven,
Nested in your eyes.
With its little razor mouth
Telling all your lies.

I hate those secret tablets
That you find so neat.
They control your future path.
They control your feet.

> Above us, in the windows,
> All the grey men shave.
> Their wives are amber puppets
> Waiting to enslave.
> It's coronary one,
> Coronary two.
> It's coronary both ways
> For me and for you.
>
> *M Baker*

MORNING ON THE FELL

I watched the sun rise early, bright and warm,
Hanging, a golden ball, above the mountain tops;
Bright clouds like huge birds
Rested their wings, caressing the highest peaks.
Below, dark shadows lay on the lower slopes,
    Hiding the rocks and trees . . .

Everywhere stillness, no lapping of the lake,
No cry of seagull, so silently gliding
    Above the dark water . . .

Then, as the sun rose and light spilled over the valley,
A sudden commotion on the fells caught my eye -
A gathering of Herdwick sheep running before a black speck,
A sheepdog, and behind, the shepherd, whistling directions,
    Moving the sheep, yet keeping them from harm . . .

And I thought of the Good Shepherd of all,
Of His gathering and keeping from harm,
In sun and shadow -
And the safe return of the lost sheep -
    As well as the ninety and nine.

Mary Dimond

FRIENDSHIP

A friend you can reach for whenever you need them
For a smile or a word or a hug
You trust them with your feelings
Your possessions and secrets
Share your heart's desires

A friend will be honest, no matter what it may be
Their thoughts you value and understand
The truth may hurt sometimes
At least for a while
But your trust in them is never denied

A friend may be distant, but only in miles
Your thoughts are with them always
The bond between you is so deep and strong
Always remembered until the end of time

Suse Lord

THE AWAKENING

they said she would watch over me
and preserve me from all harm,
so I wore my guardian angel
as if she were a charm

in a dark and anxious hour
I offered up my prayer,
but as dawn distilled the silence
I knew she could not hear

I walked alone that morning and,
for the first time in my life,
sharp terror scored my shrinking soul
like an avenging angel's knife

John Williams

Days

Today is here and present.
Today is here and now.
It has nothing to do with the crescent
of the moon jumped over by the cow.

Tomorrow is yet to come.
Tomorrow is after the night.
It may be full of fun
and laughing dogs at the sight.

But yesterday has already gone.
Yesterday is now too late.
No more childish things to don.
No more rhymes to relate.

No more *Hey Diddle Diddle!*

S A Kay

In The Dunes

Blissful early summer days!
Strolling aimlessly at ease
Like a feather in the breeze
Through the dunes on sandy ways.
Tenderly the west wind plays
Now with marram grass and heath.
All appears in perfect peace,
While we walk at quiet pace;
And the trickling sand displays
- Ephemeral memories -
For a spell still our trace.
Then these marks will fade and cease,
As we lightly leave the place
Like the feather in the breeze.

Hans-Henning Nolte

Oklahoma Sky

Early morning Oklahoma sky
I watched you change to palest grey.
I uncovered you whilst drawing
early morning curtain,
late in Oklahoma January
I had left brittle cold
English winter
and entered endless
miles of cloudy sky.
The 'plane seemed motionless
miles of
cotton woolliness
floating silently by.
Sunshine glinting
on the wings
of man-made bird
carrying lonely woman
far away from
native chills

Sylvia Lukeman

If Only

We always think there is time.
When death strikes, time stands still.
The things we always wanted to say
remain unsaid, it is too late!
If only, are the most words spoken.
As we only get one chance at life,
in reality life should be lived, as in death.

Sheila J Drewery

INTERESTING TIMES . . .? YOU MUST BE JOKING

Let me flash a signal with the headlights of a duck-boarded,
                                                                      black saloon
from cliffs high above an unknown cove on a night devoid of moon
and exchange a briefcase full of money for some micro-film or plan
to a woman, gun in her gloved hand and a tall, dark, silent man.
    And let me cross the border on a midnight, sleeping train
and meet her beside the Berlin Wall. We'd embrace in the pouring rain
and then make love with this girl called Natasha who is working for
                                                                           both sides.
I'll take a room in a hotel whose maitre'd, I know well
in this place where drudgery hides
    and not to have to wash these dishes
    and not mop the floor again
    but realise deeply held wishes
    that life's not so dull again
As I rinse away the soap-suds from the Kitchen Devil knife
I spin and stab with slash and jab to terminate his life
and cock my gun lest my enemy come and espy this awkward scene
and then I wash the Formica worktop and thoroughly degrease the hob.
You must realise that when someone dies, it's just a part of my
                                                                         other job.
So when she thinks I'm doing stir-fry I'm really speeding in pursuit
of the men in black in the gaberdine mac and the two-tone mohair suit
and in the air I lash the diamonds from a secret SS cache
I'll stake all on red now the professor's dead and she thinks I'm
                                                                   mashing mash.

H Stewart

THE WAR PARTY

There's a grey hell unfriendliness
Building from the current East:
All the cowering basement
Based ethnically correct families
Have Hollywood's dreamworks for real,
A super special effects beast,
Dropping the action dramas
From the slightly night skies.
Killing a few sacred Serbs
Though we'll be told otherwise.
The smarties only free the politicised monsters,
Those low-browed slobs
Baby eaters to a man;
Otherwise our good bombs
Wouldn't harm a fly
Or a charabanc van,
Or civil serviles in badly made flares.
Or moggies with stacked up purrs.

There's a great hell hatred
Forming in the land
A few hours travelled
From our rococo peace,
And barbecue plans.

C Butler

MARBURY MILL

There's a mill at Marbury,
  Where lives a miller's daughter,
Sheltered by many a tree,
  And swans glide on the water.

The old mill wheel is still though,
  Where rushing roaring stream ran:
Few feet tread the old bridge - low,
  Which carried many a man.

Heavy sacks were filled there, too;
  Pushing pelting corn rained down;
A warm musty smell accrued,
  Pleasant to the senses - pale brown.

Chestnuts fell on the footpath,
  Gathered by the girls and boys:
Kingfishers having a bath,
  Flashing and dipping - the joys!

Sunlight mellow on the walls;
  Waterfall tumbling bright then:
Water birds and cuckoo calls;
  On the mill pool coot and moorhen.

Herons slowly flying by;
  Strong muscles of busy men:
Those are now days long gone by.
  Ganders did not need a pen.

Smoke from twisted chimney stacks;
  Smell of cooking on the air;
Lots of hungry men for snacks;
Lawns, flowers, looked after with care.

J Millington

WHISPERINGS

The wind blew a whisper
Through my part-open door
As if to tell me a secret.
I turned around as if to see the sound.

I turned to see the gentle breeze
Blowing kisses over the trembling trees,
Then dying softly to blow the whispers
   towards another day.

I watched it caressing the flowers,
Gathering their scent into a bouquet -
To spread its sweet secret gift
Silently over a waiting world.

What privilege for me, to hear and see
The silent whispers of tranquillity.

Clare Cork

NOTE FOR ROSIE

My darling Rosie my heart is barren and bare
I've stolen and bartered, paid the boatman's fare
In a day I must be leaving you and if good God is at my side
I'll make it across the ocean upon the mercy tide.
My soul is nearly broken love, it's solemn and it's lame
No longer can I starve here, I wont play the landlord's game.
My brother and father sleep under a cruel moon
I'll not be the next sweetheart, to taste the bitter dune
If you live through this crime Rosie
Your spirit broken in and tame
You'll pass the lane where we first kissed
And your heart will shout my name.

Tony Tyrer

POETS IN REPOSE

Poets in repose, their lyrics and pompous past,
Their golden legions and wisdom cast,
With virtue, zeal, and poetic regard
Whom dreams can hurry not, nor doubts retard,
When he first didst, in his mind trace
Those divine features of a human face,
His eyes can reach those starry heights
And view the glory of Arabian nights,
Their sweet love of verse, such wealth it brings,
They'd scorn to change their state with kings.

Immortal are the hours his verse belong,
How pensive and sweet when turned to song,
If lovers yearn such sweet desires to gain
What poet would not treasure a leafy glade?
For what has made such beauty, or poets to write
But the fair paradise of nature's light,
With enduring wit, and all their worldly wise
And lustrous passion that never dies,
In spacious halls he strayed, and bowers few,
He was a poet for sure, and a lover too.

All verses long and many more
His mind was born with poetic lore,
These are the living pleasures of a poet's mind
Whose words are images of thoughts refined,
Their wisdom gone by, and they to heaven up-flown
Lulled with rhyme and verses known,
All poets young with inspiration, must
Consign to verse, or come to dust,
If you the poets look upon these verse
Do not so much, my name rehearse.

John Leighton

My Evening Mail

I read the paper with great care
There's always something special there
Perhaps something I ant to buy
A new recipe for me to try
Which shop is having a sale?
It's all found in The Evening Mail.
The local news is in there too
And people with their points of view
What's on the television it tells
Who is hearing wedding bells
If you want a house or car
The paper tells you where they are
When the hour goes off or on
You'll find it showing on page one
The crossword passes time away
I like my paper every day.

M P John

Blue Hour

In the blue hour of evening
the poet puts her song aside
and lays her pen to rest.
In the blue hour of evening
she drinks from a well of words
and bathes in the clear water
of many friendly voices.
In the blue hour of evening
ideas settle in her mind - boats
drawn up on a silver beach.

Michael Collins

DEATH OF A GREAT

As the deep rich tone of the clarinet
Lingered across the churchyard
Anger ran through my body,
Anger towards a man that's dead.

He killed himself, that's all I know
And this wasn't his time to go.
If only he'd listened to what we said.
He might still be alive, alive and not dead.

He wouldn't listen. He knew best.
He said, I'll live longer than the rest.
But like most jazz artists he didn't think,
Got mixed up in drugs and drink.

That's why I'm mad, know it's not right,
He just gave up without a fight.
he could have done it but he never tried.
He was stubborn and had too much pride.

Playing with Rob, both sat on the stage,
A special moment I'll never forget -
Junior Hayton and Crazy Cat Melville
Such a perfect duet.

'Ain't Misbehavin' the song that we played,
Using no written score,
Tapping out the crazy beat
On a hard wooden floor.

He's probably up there jamming with the greats
Rockin' and a knockin' at those pearly gates.
So thanks old pal for being there for me
Rob Melville RIP.

Jaron Hayton

STERILE ENVIRONMENT

Today's the day it happens, I've never felt so ill,
It's alright them all saying, I can no longer take the pill.
Twenty years of pill pushing, I've knocked back a few score,
But never whilst I took the pill, did it ever make me sore,
They are going to sterilise me through two tiny little holes!
One's inside my navel, through some microscopic poles!
'Turn up at eight-thirty, and we'll show you to a bed.'
The thought of what they are gonna do, is screwing up my head.
My bag is packed, it's ready, which is more than I can say.
I just wish I could erase, this op on me today.
My tummy's really churning, and every time it aches,
I think about how sore I'll be when my body finally wakes.
The taxi's here it's time now, there's nothing I can do,
I must pull myself together, come on, I've got to see it through.
Arrived on time so frightened.
'Dear do you feel alright?'
'Yes,' I said, so timidly, 'I've just had a bad night.'
Next thing I'm in my nightie, tucked up in a bed.
With only *operation,* buzzing in my head.
'The trolley has arrived for you, just you climb on board
And before you know it, you'll be back up on the ward.'
Wrapped up in a blanket, trundled off to the unknown,
I felt so defenceless, and completely on my own.
They parked me by the theatre door, with people dressed in green.
Then injected me with some liquid, that's the last thing I had seen.
I remember hearing voices, but they were far away,
Next think there were nurses, and I looked to hear them say.
'Awake at last? Thank goodness! Do you not want to go?
Your huband's phoned, he'll pick you up in an hour or so.'
To think how much I'd worried, the doctor she was right.
Operation over, and the pain was only slight.

Kazzie Ingram

MY ANGEL

I stand on the edge, I dare not see,
The light on the water, taking over me.

I cannot resist, the feelings too strong,
I hesitate, could it go wrong?

I draw back from the edge and say a prayer,
Oh why, oh why do I really care?

I need to rest, to ease my mind,
There's answers I really need to find.

My mind plays tricks, I need to go,
My breath is shallow, my heart is low.

Then an angel calls out to me,
I look around and there I see,

A hand so pure as the driven snow,
Then in an instance, I seem to know.

As I, upon this earth do tread,
I need not feel fear or dread.

For even in my most darkest hour,
My Angel, my strength, my power.

Dawn Graham

LIES AND TRUTH

You
You sympathise
You free my eyes
So we see lies and truth
You see my youth
You see my shy nature
You see my willingness to waste time
Filling my head with nonsense
You see this fence I sit upon
Deciding which side to fall
Whilst I see small things
You see hugeness
Sting me with those songs you sing
Bring me peace
Release my second self
Show me change
Rearrange my thoughts into coherent language
Chain them into place
You see my face
My reflection
Dissecting space into fragments of time
You find my mind behind disguise
Sigh my sighs
You free my eyes
So we see lies and truth.

Melvyn Hampson

UNIFORM

We all wear a uniform
Though on some it's more obvious than others
The chains
The torn remains of a denim jacket
The suit the smart look
The handkerchief in the breast pocket
Do the rough looks imply
A harsher life
With no care, no responsibilities?
Or do we prejudge,
Forgetting that appearances can be deceiving
And on the surface
It's just a uniform after all?

Clive Euston